DARE TO BE MAGNIFICENT

The Five Key Elements of An
Unshakable Extraordinary Life

Unlock Your Personal Power
Change Your Life & Thrive

Joseph McClendon III

DARE TO BE MAGNIFICENT

Ordering Information & Quantity Sales: Special discounts are available on quantity purchases by corporations, associations, and others. For details, contact the publisher. Orders by U.S. & International trade bookstores and wholesalers at: info@abundantpress.com. Printed in the United States of America- Library of Congress-in-Publication Data. Please note: This book was put together very quickly for a conference, so if you find errors, like spelling or grammar, please send us an email.

Title: Dare to Be Magnificent

Sub-title: The Five Key Elements Of Living an Unshakable Extraordinary Life - Unlock Your Personal Power Change Your Life & Thrive

Author: Joseph McClendon III

The main category of the book — Lifestyle - Entrepreneurship - Business - Personal Development

First Edition, First Printing 9-01-2020

ISBN: 978-1-948287-19-7

Get access to additional free resources:
JosephMcClendon.com

Disclaimer

The information within this book is intended as reference material only and not as medical or professional advice. Information contained herein is intended to give you the tools to make informed decisions about your wellness, lifestyle, and physical and mental health.

It should not be used as a substitute for any treatment that has been prescribed or recommended by your doctor. The information within this book must not be construed as a medical, therapeutic, or psychological treatment, nor are any such claims made.

Every reasonable effort has been made to ensure that the material within this book is true, correct, complete, and appropriate at the time of writing. Nevertheless, the authors do not accept responsibility for any omission or error, or for any injury, damage, loss, or financial consequences arising from the use of this material.

The authors, promoters, and publishers are not healthcare professionals, and expressly disclaim any responsibility for any adverse effects occurring as a result of the use of the suggestions or information herein. This material is offered as practical, current information available about disease and health management for your own education and enjoyment.

If you suspect you have a disease of any kind, it is imperative that you seek medical attention. It is also recommended that you consult with a qualified healthcare professional before beginning any diet or exercise program.

By accepting this information, you agree to hold Joseph McClendon III, his associates, partners, and affiliates free of liability and damage, and you proceed on your own free will. You and you alone are solely responsible for the results that you produce. Do not continue unless you fully agree to these terms and conditions.

Thank You.
Now Let's Get Real.

TABLE OF CONTENTS

Foreword

Les Brown

Hello, I'm Les Brown. You may know me as a motivational speaker, a former television host and radio DJ, or even for the years I spent representing the 29th District of Ohio in the U.S. Congress. However you know me, there's something I want you to know.

You have something special. You have greatness in you.

In today's environment of uncertainty and fear, tens of thousands of people are losing their lives around our nation. Businesses are going under. Millions of people are unemployed and homeless. Millions are feeling hopeless, powerless, and uncertain about their future.

Now, more than ever, we need a book that can help us navigate these treacherous waters. We must know that this trial has not come to stay: it has come to pass.

If you are experiencing any of these feelings, you are not alone. Millions of others are there with you. And my dear friend, Joseph McClendon III, has written this book for all of you.

As you read through its pages, prepare to be catapulted from your current mindset into the life that you hunger for and deserve.

The strategies that Joseph McClendon III has shared with the thousands of people he has trained over the years are timely, transformative, dynamic and powerful. His strategies are proven to connect with the highest level of your being.

Joseph teaches you how to create a life based on:

1. Accepting the magnitude of your life's purpose, and

2. Allowing your unique Magnificence to be demonstrated in everything that you do.

I can personally attest to the effectiveness of Joseph's training because he is one of the few leaders whom I consider to be a personal mentor. He is a good man.

He and I developed an instant future at our first meeting years ago. I felt a deep connection to his story about his father and the impact that his father had on building the greatness that he had within him. Like all of us, he had to overcome tragedies in life in order to be triumphant. His father prepared him for this even before he became a man.

And now, he is going to share these great gifts his father gave him with us.

His years of self-study and self-evolution have made him a master at bringing out the best in others. All of us can learn from Joseph's experiences. Even as a well-known motivational speaker myself, I'm still learning.

I am so glad that Joseph wrote this book and is sharing his many nuggets and intellectual gold like only he can. Like me, Joseph was transformed by hearing a voice that changed the trajectory of his life.

If you are struggling to overcome any kind of challenge in life, Joseph's voice and his story can lift you up. He can show you the way through. I know, because this book has accomplished that for me.

This book is for those who are on top, and for those who want to get there.

As you read these pages, I urge you to take notes and implement these best practices. He knows what he is doing.

Joseph is not a man who practices what he preaches. Instead, he preaches what he practices. And that is why he is so authentic.

Your life of Magnificence is awaiting you if you have the hunger to step into your greatness.

I encourage you to allow *Dare To Be Magnificent* to help you reclaim your life to help you become the greatest version of yourself.

You have something special. You are an unrepeatable miracle.

If you are willing to break out of the cage of self-doubt and fear like Joseph and I did, you will find the keys to free yourself in this timely, Magnificent book whose time has come.

You have something special. You have greatness in you.

This book will find the people who need it. From my lips to God's ears. This has been Les Brown, Mrs. Mamie Brown's baby boy.

Les Brown

Introduction

From the Desk of Joseph McClendon III

As I am writing this book in the summer of 2020, the streets are still filled with hundreds of thousands of people marching for justice and racial equality. The awareness of the importance of kindness, caring, and understanding is truly astounding. The same media outlets that have kept us frightened and uncertain have inadvertently given us reason for introspection and compassion for our fellow man.

As evidenced by the diverse cultural and ethnic mix of beautiful souls filling the streets, our differences are becoming less and less critical and our similarities are shining through. On the surface, I am encouraged to see efforts to make changes in our legal and governmental institutions that might bring about more fair and just conditions for all.

It has now been 96 days since life turned on a dime for all of us. It's the first time in a century that one disease has affected the entire planet. There have been pandemics and plagues and infectious diseases that have affected large parts of the earth, but never one that brought our modern world to a screeching halt like this one. Entire countries have shut down, economies have collapsed, businesses have been put on hold, and livelihoods have been lost forever.

Just when it seemed that the worst was upon us, another black man was murdered in plain sight in the streets by law enforcement, igniting a powder keg that has been compacting for four centuries.

The truth is, infectious diseases are nothing new. They happen all the time. And sadly, murders of African Americans by law-enforcement are nothing new either. They occur with a high frequency that, until recently, 83% of the population either wasn't aware of or chose to turn a blind eye to.

The difference this time is that everything played out in real-time, in living color and horrifying sound and 4K vision, 24/7, on our flatscreens and handheld devices.

That, combined with institutional leadership challenges and fear-based decision-making on the part of those in power, set the stage for a catastrophic shift in life as we knew it. All of these elements coming together at this juncture have forced us to rethink our beliefs about ourselves, about other people, and about the world we live in.

While it is clear that this awakening has brought out the worst in some human beings and their horrific behaviors, it's also clear that it has brought to the surface some of the best in our human nature and human behavior. The outpouring of love and compassion is truly epic and astounding. As a civilization, our evolution is unfolding right before our eyes.

This Too Shall Pass.

Hopefully, by the time you read this book, we will be well on our way to the next stage of higher thinking and consciousness. It's critical to recognize that this is one of the many ebbs and flows of life itself.

This is an inescapable physical and metaphysical fact of life. Winter always follows fall, spring always follows winter, and summer always follows spring. Knowing and remembering what has happened in the past better equips us with the tools to predict what will happen in the future.

The ability to anticipate gives us the ability to plan how to best capitalize on this flow, as long as our anticipation is based on empirical evidence collected from the past. The deck is heavily stacked in our favor if we make the right decisions about what to do in the present—being fully aware that we have this option and this skill set. The decisions we make are like money in the bank regarding what is possible for our future.

Uncertainty and confusion are rampant around the world, more at this moment than at any time in recent history. Those of us who dare to dream while the rest of the world has an uncertain nightmare will not only create the abundance that we desire; we will also become the beacons of possibility and hope for those seeking leadership, guidance, and a plan.

Certainty is a skill, and all skills can be learned and mastered. But certainty also comes from knowledge and experience. Success builds on success. You only move to the next rung on the ladder after moving through the previous step.

We have all had countless successes in our lives to build upon. We've all had a myriad of experiences that gave us certainty in our lives. If you've experienced certainty once, you can experience it again. You can use these past victories to cultivate and grow your certainty about any and everything you want to be, do, achieve, and have.

You are Magnificence

Listen. I might not know you personally yet, but I know that you have dreams, goals, and desires. I may not know what they are *yet*. But I know this to my core: no matter what your dream is, no matter what obstacles, setbacks, discouragements, and roadblocks you have endured, those desires you are holding in your soul are uniquely yours. And yes: they are possible. They are attainable, and you deserve them.

Obtaining them will involve changing your habits, thoughts, beliefs, surroundings, and even your body. This is required to change your life and its trajectory. Don't get it twisted. Changing your life is not effortless or easy. But the rewards will be magical and fulfilling.

It's not always easy, but it can be simple. And life is much, much simpler than we have been led to believe. The process of molding your life to fit your dreams is an epic story that you will tell your children and then to your grandchildren.

If it were easy, everybody would do it. But it's not, and that's why people don't. It's why you encounter opposition, rejection, pain, and setbacks when you come face-to-face with doubt and uncertainty. It's why you stumble at the altar of discipline. It's why you question the heavens as to why you are being singled out and tested. It's why you stand frustrated and broken, wondering why this is happening to only you.

At these times, remember this simple fact: every single obstacle, all of them—yes, *all of them*—are just different forms of fear. They are placed in your path to test you, strengthen you, grow your character, and ensure that you deserve what you desire.

We don't grow when things are easy; we only grow when things are difficult. If you're going through hell, *keep going*.

But how?

Decide right here, right now, at this very moment that you will endure the storms—no matter what.

Stay true to your soul and step up. Rise above your nemesis and claim your victory early.

That is why you picked up this book. You have chosen to *Dare to be Magnificent.*

Hard times are going to come, but they are only temporary. They too shall pass. They can't stay. They leave when they're denied the nutrition they crave. They fade when they're starved of your attention and energy.

Magnificence is not rare, it is not fickle, and it is not elusive. It's not some unattainable quality placed in front of you to tease and torment you with its mystery. But it is selective, and it will not show its glorious face and share its bounty with you just because you open the door and invite it in.

Let me let you in on a little secret. The truth of the matter is, Magnificence already let itself into your home a long time ago. It lives in every one of us and every cell in your body.

It came with the package called life. It followed you when you came kicking and screaming into this world and it will stay with you for the entire run. It's critical that you believe that you are the one, and *now is your time.*

You are not 'one of the ones'; you are *The One.* And your time is not someday, but *this time!* Right. NOW!

You are the one and only genuine real deal. There is not and never will be another just like you. My dear friend and brilliant mentor, Victor Lamont Wooten, says:

> "What if you were given a one-of-a-kind Diamond? It is the only one like it on the planet. It is bigger and better and brighter than anything you've ever seen and more precious than any diamond in all of creation.
>
> "Would you cherish that diamond? How would you take care of it? How would you feel about its value and its rarity? Of course you'd cherish it and protect it. You'd be so proud of it.
>
> "Well, that diamond is the true you. Your true self is just like that diamond. And *you* deserve your praise, adoration, and protection."

Sadly, most people will never meet their true selves. Yes, they will live. Yes, they will have fun. But they will work, they will make a living and settle for less than they truly desire. They will live with the quiet numbness of complacency. And as they close in all too quickly on the end of their lives, never knowing that they could have had it all, they will sigh in quiet disappointment, knowing that they left so much undone and unachieved.

They stopped growing; they stopped working on themselves. Or worse yet, they never even started. They opted for the illusion of long-term comfort instead of stretching themselves and welcoming the short-term discomfort that ensures long-term abundance. They never even knew that if they had done the hard stuff in the short term, they would have had an easier life. Instead, they opted to do the easy stuff and, as a result, lived a hard life.

Many people find solace in complaining. They complain because they are afraid to do something. They don't want to risk being uncomfortable to change their situations.

Why? Because procrastination, hesitation, fear of failure, fear of success, complacency, laziness, apathy, sarcasm, pessimism, worry, and doubt are all thieves of our dreams. They are just as damaging as drugs or alcohol or any other destructive substance that you could put in your body.

Hard work, practice, disciple, and struggle are not your enemy. They are your allies, your ride-along, your tools. They help thicken your skin. They're the best teachers to make sure that you step up and win. They are there to warn you and to challenge you to shape your will and character into exactly what is needed to become the best version of you.

You've already spent too much time worrying about what other people think of you. Whether they like you or approve of you. You've invested more time and emotion in them than you have yourself. You know more about them than you know about your precious self.

Well, let me let you in on a little secret: 80% of the time, those other people are just as scared as you are and just as worried about what others think as your silly butt is. And the other 20% of people—they simply don't care. Most of the time, they're not even thinking about you.

Listen. What others think about you is none of your business when it comes to building your confidence and strengthening your self-worth. Nobody cares what you *don't* do. Nobody cares if you don't stick to your diet, or don't make enough money, or don't get that new car or make the grade.

When you step up, they care. When you show up bad to the bone and get things done, they care. When you make a difference and do something for the good of the community—then, those other people care.

I dare you to step in front of you. I challenge you to spend one full day just with your thoughts and feelings. Dig deep and get to know who you really are.

That's what you are about to do with this book. We're not going to get to know the 'you' that you think you should be, or the 'you' that you used to be. We're going to get to know who you are *right now*. The good, the bad, and the beautiful.

As ye seek, so shall ye find, and quickly. As ye seek, ye shall find ye.

It's then, and only then, that you level the playing field and go toe-to-toe with the only thing that can stop you: you.

It's then that you will recognize that you are and always have been the Magnificent champion you have been searching for. It is then that you set the stakes in the ground that mark the beginning of your reign of Magnificence.

For those who dare to dream, while the rest of the world is having a nightmare, life will yield an extraordinary bounty. You shall not only inherit the prosperity that you seek. You will also be a shining example of what is possible. You will be in a position to help lead the masses to freedom.

You are one of the mighty leaders of the free world. When you become the you that you are meant to be, you are set apart. You might find that your existing relationships begin to change. It might seem lonely at first. But you will quickly recognize that you are surrounded by like-minded and like-spirited people who are moving with purpose and joy. And together, you will make change happen.

Dare to make your life Magnificent. Dare to step outside of the circle of ordinary life. Dare to hold your vision in plain sight.

Not everybody will see it. Most will never even know you weren't by their side as they blindly slipped into the comfort of mediocrity. People who are living their desires will attract winners to surround themselves with and attach themselves to.

The people living their dreams are the people who know that if it's going to happen, it's up to them.

You must know that you are not typical. You are not common. You are a freak. A freak of nature, in that nature will support you as you step off into the unknown just as the wind rushes in to lift the eagle's wings. Life will rush in to support you in your endeavor to be Magnificent.

Lastly, I want you to know that I don't teach theory. I won't teach something that I have not already done for myself. I won't teach something that I have not taught before and attained amazing results.

I am about to share with you the gift of my greatest mentors and teachers. These are the words, lessons, and influences of the people who taught me from the very beginning how to *Dare to be Magnificent*. My sincerest and deepest wish is that you had, have, or will have, someone like them to guide and mentor you.

If you don't, then I humbly offer my service and my mentors' wisdom to you. Please accept my gift in the spirit that it is meant.

To be Magnificent is to magnify who you already are. It's critical that you know that you are already amazing.

You were made to shine. You are blessed and you are beautiful. Dare to be

MAGNIFICENT.

CHAPTER 1

Opening the Door to Magnificence

"You already are the magnificence that you seek."
— Gail Lynne Goodwin

"The time to embrace your magnificence is now."
— Rhonda Byrne

When most people think of the word *Magnificence*, they think of a finished product. An object, or maybe even a situation or event, that is looked upon with appreciation and awe for what it has already become.

There is Magnificence in a beautiful sunset or sunrise. There is Magnificence in all of God's creations. There is Magnificence in a musical performance by a virtuoso pianist, a Picasso painting, or one of Michelangelo's breathtaking marble sculptures.

Perhaps a better understanding or description of the word Magnificence is 'to magnify the very essence of a thing.'

I think we can all agree that when Dr. Martin Luther King, Jr. delivered his famous "I Have a Dream" speech on the steps of the Lincoln Memorial in Washington DC in 1963 his performance was Magnificent. His words painted pictures in our minds and touched our hearts and souls. It is one of the greatest speeches and deliveries in history.

But did you know that Dr. King delivered that same speech dozens of times before he spoke those words on that glorious day? Did you know that he rehearsed that speech over and over again until it became a natural extension of who he was?

Most of us never think about the hours and days and maybe weeks that it took him to write the speech. Let alone the countless times he performed it in front of live audiences while acquiring the necessary experience to deliver it the way that he did on August 28, 1963.

Dr. Martin Luther King, Jr. took what he had experienced throughout his life and molded it into something that forever changed the landscape of the planet. He took the essence of who he was as a man and magnified it with his words, his mannerisms, and his heart.

I submit to you that inside of you already is a level of Magnificence that you are probably unaware of. It came with a package called life. As you came kicking and screaming into this world, you brought with you a spark, energy, power, and abundant spirit.

Yes, my dear friend, the very essence of God came along for the ride. Now the magnification process is at hand.

How do we magnify what we were born with?

There's A Penny In Your Pocket

When I was about eight years old, my father called me outside to help him work on the car. This was a regular weekend occurrence with us because our 1960 Dodge station wagon was on its last leg. We didn't have a lot of money, so my father would do all the car repairs himself. He was a mechanic in the United States Air Force and he worked on huge C130 transports and cargo aircraft, so cars were a piece of cake for him.

Up until that point, my role was just to hand him a wrench or a screwdriver or to hold something when he needed it. My father made it a point to always teach me something while he was working.

To be honest, I wasn't really paying that much attention most of the time. He never complained or swore or got frustrated with the tasks. He even seemed to enjoy whatever it was that he was doing. He would tell me stories and jokes and he would always explain what he was doing and why he was doing it.

Earlier that day, my mom had had some trouble getting the car started. She turned the key and a loud clicking sound came from the engine. Even though the car eventually started, my dad said it was a clear sign that sooner or later something was going to go wrong, and we could wind up stranded somewhere on the side of the road. We only had one car, so it was critical that we kept it in working condition.

"Never wait," he would always say. "At the first sign of trouble, attack it and handle it right away. Never give trouble a chance to get on even footing."

Even before we started, my father told me that the problem was in the starter and we needed to remove this part of the car to fix it.

Then he said, "Pay real close attention this time, son, because you're going to learn a lifelong lesson."

Truth be told, he said that a lot, about a lot of things we did. But this time he seemed even more intense and serious. I dug in deep and tried my best to pay attention and make sense of what he said, and I kept a lookout for something special in the task at hand.

We jacked the car up, disconnected all of the electrical cables, unbolted the starter, and removed it from the engine. After about an hour and a half, we were staring at this big greasy contraption of gears and wires. I remember it being so heavy and awkward that I could hardly lift it.

The starter looked worn out, and even at eight years old I assumed that we were just going to throw that one out, go to the parts store, and buy another starter. After all, this one was dirty, greasy, and broken.

My dad, on the other hand, had other plans. He said that a new starter would cost us close to $40 and we didn't have that kind of money to spare. He said, "We'll just fix it ourselves."

Then, like a surgeon doing a heart transplant, he took that starter apart right there on the workbench in the garage. He cleaned it up and undid all of the wires and cables. It turned out that the reason the starter was not turning the engine was that a little copper washer about the size of a penny had worn out.

"Watch this," he said. Then he reached in his pocket and took out a single copper penny. He laid it next to the worn-out washer to see that they were both the same in diameter and thickness. Then he drilled a hole in that penny and made his own copper washer. He proceeded to put the starter back together using the new penny as a washer while explaining to me where each nut and bolt went.

I was blown away. Not only did my dad remember where all the pieces and the parts went, but it went back together faster than it came apart. He put the starter back in the engine. We lowered the car to the ground and it started up right away.

Then my dad asked me, "What questions do you have about what just happened?"

I had several questions. "Dad, how did you know the washer was the problem? How did you know how to fix it? Have you done this before?"

He laughed. "No, I haven't. But when you know the fundamental elements of how things work, you can apply them to anything. Because I learned about mechanics, I know that mechanics apply to everything. And I had a penny. I saved us money, I saved us time, and we had a good time, didn't we?"

I nodded.

"You don't have to know everything," he explained. "You just have to know the fundamentals. You don't have to have a lot, either. Oftentimes if you look hard enough, you'll find that you already have what you need to make the changes you want.

"Whenever something happens and you have to do something, anything at all," he continued, "ask yourself: 'What do I already know and what do I already have that I can use to succeed at whatever it is that I'm doing?' You just have to know the fundamental elements and you can do just about anything and be successful at anything you want to do.

"Take what you know and use it to get what you want. And that which you don't know you can learn and use it in combination with what you do know."

The great Jim Rohn, the Foremost Personal Achievement Philosopher and one of the greatest motivators and speakers of all times once said:

> *"Success in life is not about mastering everything. There are just a handful of principles that make the biggest difference in what you will and won't do and achieve."*

In the spirit of my father and Mr. Rohn, I'm going to show you a handful of things—five things, to be exact—that when you place them into your psyche, your life will become even more Magnificent.

Life Is Much Simpler Than We've Been Led To Believe

Daddy did it with a penny. And now, you're going to do it with your life. Take what you already have, and use it. I'm going to show you how to take a handful of things that you already have and use them to magnify your life to create Magnificence.

You're about to enter your own world and find out once and for all exactly how you function. Then you'll learn how to use that information to get the very best out of yourself. You're going to meet some amazing people—people just like you—who wanted a change and made it happen.

Most importantly, you are going to set in motion a chain of actions that will help you bring about physical, mental, and emotional change.

It is my honor to share with you the five fundamental elements that make up the foundation of every person who has achieved greatness. And the best part is, you already possess them at some level.

Together, we are going to learn *what* they are, *where* they are, *how* to pull them out, and finally, *how* to use them to enhance your own greatness and Magnificence.

I know this sounds like a bold statement. But as you watch, listen and apply what I'm about to share with you, you'll find that you hold within yourself the power to create and sustain great health, great energy, great wellness, and great abundance.

We All Want It All

Here's how things truly are. I believe that most people want to be in tip-top physical shape, to look as good as they can, to feel as good as they can, and to be wealthy and happy. But very few actually accomplish it. The global average is about 2.7 to 3%.

If you're reading this book, you obviously want some of those things. But a 3% success rate might not look promising.

Well, here is the good news: we've all had experiences in our lives where we were operating "in the zone," where we lived and functioned at our optimum levels.

I'm going to show you how to master being in the zone, even if we have to go back to your early childhood to capture it and bring it to the now.

If you have done it before, you can do it again. And you can magnify it.

Don't believe me? *Just watch!*

My Story

Please allow me to share with you a little about my life, and how I came to learn and apply these elements to work for myself and for others.

I was born in Fort Campbell, Kentucky. I was the second child of Mr. and Mrs. Joseph McClendon, Jr.. I was named after my grandfather, Joseph McClendon, Sr. I had one older sister, Ava Jean. Over the next six years, my parents had two more children: Anita Joy and Lisa Jannette, making us a family of six.

My parents were extraordinary. At the time I was born, neither of them had a college education and they were raising us at a time in the United States when life difficult for black families (*yes, even more than now*), they instilled in us a belief that times would change and that we were good, intelligent, and worthy—no matter what other people told us about the color of our skin.

My father joined the United States Air Force as a teenager to escape the mean streets of New York and to serve his country. My mother was a former opera singer who had attended the Juilliard School for music. They kept us clean, well-mannered, and focused. They stressed the importance of educating and improving ourselves.

Probably the most important thing they taught us was to be *self-reliant*. Being self-sufficient was a must in the McClendon family. I remember doing dishes and chores as young as six years old. This lesson served a very practical purpose: We could not necessarily count on others to help us, so we had to get used to doing everything for ourselves.

Like many of us, I've had some terrible things happen in my life. At one point in my life, I experienced a series of racially motivated incidents that devastated me and robbed me of my self-esteem, my self-worth, and all of the essential elements that I had once possessed.

As a result, I found myself homeless and hopeless. With seemingly nowhere to turn, my life was spiraling out of control fast. I was secretly angry, resentful, and ashamed. But the person I was most angry with was myself.

I was angry because I couldn't figure out how to win. I was angry at myself because I wasn't living the kind of life that I was raised to live. I couldn't find the solution to my own inner torment. I was resentful because I know that I was buying into my own negative opinions and self-sabotage.

I was embarrassed to show my face because, in my eyes, I had become such a failure. I felt that anyone who knew me knew how much potential I had. And if they saw how far I had fallen, they would judge me like I was judging myself. They'd reject me.

All of this was going on in my head and I was going crazy because I didn't know how to stop it.

People Care

Fortunately, someone cared enough to reach out to me and offer me a hand. A kind person, someone that I didn't know and who didn't know me, introduced me to a different way of thinking and being. A different way of believing in myself, other people, and the world around me.

He gave me the book *Think and Grow Rich* by Napoleon Hill. Because of the elements my father instilled in me at a very young age—the same elements I am about to share with you—I didn't *just* read the book. I *devoured* it. I did the exercises. As a result, my life changed. This book taught me to do things differently and approach life from a whole new perspective.

If I had not been given The Five Essential Elements of Greatness by my father, the words in *Think and Grow Rich* might have fallen on deaf ears. At most, I might have dabbled and given up like I imagine most people who read that book do.

Contrary to popular belief, knowledge is not power. Knowledge is only information. And all of us have an abundance of information. Without the internal fortitude to keep in play those emotions and thoughts that fuel our *actions*, we default to the path of least resistance no matter how much knowledge we have.

And unfortunately, that path of least resistance has become more and more enticing with all of the distractions that are thrust into our line of sight. There are countless distractions, doubts, and other messages set before us each day which can permeate our conscious and unconscious minds. Discipline of thought and *action* is necessary to continue driving towards our goal undeterred.

These five elements my father taught me saved my life. When I went back to thank the stranger who gifted me *Think and Grow Rich* for what he had done for me, I asked him: "How do I repay you?"

What he told me changed my life even more.

"Do the same thing I did for you for as many people as you possibly can." he told me. "Do this for the rest of your life. That's how you repay me."

And that's why I'm writing this book. That's why I'm going to give you the gift of these five elements.

I was raised by two remarkable parents. The lessons they taught me allowed me to have these five elements at my fingertips all my life.

With your permission, I'll share those lessons and elements with you so that you may take them and thrive.

Together, we will make the world a better place.

Straight Up!

I want to talk to you about what this book is about, what you can expect, how to proceed, and how to get the best results from this time we have together.

First, I'll share with you a little bit about myself and what qualifies me to even be talking to you now. Then we will get started on the work of magnifying your Magnificent essence.

I was first inspired to write this book by my dear friend and mentor Leslie Calvin, known to many of you as Les Brown.

Unless you've been living under a rock, you know that Les is an international treasure. He has been inspiring and empowering people for decades. He's responsible for changing the lives of millions and millions of people around the world. If you have ever had the opportunity to be around him, you know that his electricity is unmatched.

Just being around him makes you feel that anything is possible. When you hear him speak, you know that it is. He's one of the wisest people I know and he cares so deeply that you feel it just by his presence.

For years, Les and I have wanted to do something together. With everything happening in the world around us, we have decided that NOW is that time.

We've talked about what is available and what is missing in people's lives that keep them from achieving their dreams, goals, and desires. We've talked about what is needed and what is necessary in this day and age to help people go further faster. We've talked about how many people who want and desire to have a better life are struggling to break the bonds of mediocrity.

The end result of these conversations is this book.

During our conversations, Les asked me what I thought it was that made me so different. Why I had such a high level of drive and accomplishment. What made me so passionate and determined. And how that led to my successes in business, my physical body, my lifestyle, and my happiness.

He asked me what this difference was and where it came from. He asked me where my passion to share with others came from. We discussed many vague principles and ideas, but struggled to pinpoint one specific factor that was different in my life from the lives of most people.

Then, Les asked me who was the biggest influence on my life as a child.

It came to me like a bolt of lightning. It was a no brainer.

"My father," I said.

I learned how to be how I am from the greatest man I have ever known—Senior Master Sergeant Joseph McClendon, Jr..

He didn't just tell me how to be. He taught me by his example. My father was a great man, a Magnificent man, and not just because I say so. He was Magnificent because of how he lived and how he impacted me and the other people around him.

My father lived a life that will outlive him through me, and through other people's lives that he touched.

I want you to write this down. I highly recommend that you take notes while reading this book, for reasons that will soon become obvious. There will be exercises, specific steps, and important ideas shared here that can transform your daily life if you apply them on a daily basis.

But for now, I want you to start by writing this down to honor my father's memory:

The five elements of greatness are takeaways from Joseph McClendon, Jr..

I also want you to write this down:

I know that you have Magnificence in you, just as my father knew that I had Magnificence in me.

How To Get The Most Out Of This Book

This book is a process designed to produce lasting, tangible changes in your life. My assumption is that you picked up this book because you desire to change. You want a change in behavior that will produce a change in your lifestyle; a change in your emotions that will produce more joy, certainty, self-esteem, and confidence.

Perhaps you are not sure what it is that you ultimately desire—you just know you want more.

If you only *read* this book, you will receive knowledge and information. It will make sense to you, and maybe you'll become smarter.

But knowledge is not what changes you. Most people already know way more than they actually need to know in order to get what they want. Virtually everyone who is overweight and desires to become thin *knows* how to lose weight. But they don't *act* on what they know.

Action, application, and execution is where true power lies. In the information age, it is not *just* what we know: it's whether we *act* reliably based on what we know.

It's that simple.

This book is a step-by-step system to not only teach you what my father taught me, but to ensure that you *act* on this knowledge. The more you act on it, the more confidence, skill, and results you will build. The more you act on this knowledge, the easier it will become to do so every day until you have transformed your entire life.

In this book you will read and learn, and then you will do exercises. For the most part, the exercises will be as simple as listing or writing something down. But *do* take the time to do them.

Reading this book without doing the exercises is exactly like knowing how to lose weight, but not putting that knowledge into action. It will not get you the results that you want.

Understand that change happens through the physical and mental action of participating in the process.

Just as action can build muscle, it also builds neural pathways in your brain. Writing down new words will literally create new paths in your brain, which open up new doorways of thought, action, and emotion. Once these pathways are created, we will see how to strengthen them through practice until they become your new *habits*. In this way, you can intentionally shape your habits and your whole life.

By completing these exercises, you will be systematically rewiring your brain to think differently. You will be causing yourself to feel differently, and this in turn will cause you to *do* things differently and ultimately produce better results.

It is the searching for answers and the movement of your body as you write and speak that rewires your brain.

You don't have to understand exactly what we are doing in order to get results. *You just need to do it.*

The honeybee doesn't even know that it is pollinating the flowers as it goes from plant to plant. It just performs its process of gathering food, knowing that the process feels good.

Think of yourself as a honeybee collecting yummy morsels from this book. To really get that nectar, you must spend some time completing the exercises, just as a honeybee must spend some time resting on each flower.

You know there is a deeper, more powerful phenomenon taking place as you do these exercises. But the *doing* is even more important than that knowledge.

I know that total life transformation is possible in a short amount of time. I know because I've done it myself.

I've had high highs and low lows, but I don't let either define me. Yes, I've been wealthy and wildly successful in finance, but that's not what this is all about.

This book is about developing yourself into the person you know you were meant to be. It's about living the life of your dreams.

Each day can be filled with an unimaginable, contagious, crazy joy if you're willing to take the steps!

When I'm doing seminars, I often ask the audience how many of them have read the book *Think and Grow Rich*. Because of the nature of what I do, many people who are attracted to my seminars have also come across this Magnificent book. Usually, about 45 to 60% of my audience has read the book.

I then ask how many of them enjoyed the book and got a lot out of it? All of the hands stay up. Next I ask, "How many of you believe that the lessons in that book can change your life?" And of course, all of the hands stay up.

Finally, I ask: "How many of you did the exercises in the book?"

There's always an audible sigh of nervous laughter in the audience after I ask that question. About 80% of their hands drop. And it's my guess that 90% of those whose hands remain up just aren't being honest. The reality is that most people read, but don't do what is required of them to get the results that the book suggests.

If I were to ask "How many of you *became rich* because you read that book?", my guess is that the hands staying up would be the hands of the people *who actually did the book's exercises.*

Because of the elements that were instilled in me, I tend to do what is asked of me. I tend to follow through and be disciplined about things. My father did not merely *tell* me how important it was to take the necessary small actions that lead to success: he showed me. After watching him save $40 by replacing a washer with a penny, how could I fail to understand the importance small actions could have to getting results in life?

I received *Think and Grow Rich* from a stranger named Albert who insisted that I do the exercises. His insistence, combined with the desperate circumstances in my life, caused me to actually *do* all of the exercises, one-by-one as the book directed. As a result I started to see very, very rapid changes in myself and in my environment.

The point of all this is, it is critical that you do the exercises that I'm about to share with you.

I want you to treat this book like a user's manual for the human condition. My suggestion is that you read the chapters, reread the chapters, and then do the exercises as they are laid out for you.

The following are a set of principles and suggestions that you can follow to get the very best out of this book. They will help you to emerge triumphant in your change.

When it is all said and done, I'm going to show you exactly how to function as a human being. I'm going to show you how to use that information to get the absolute best out of yourself.

I want you to realize that it might not always seem like these exercises are moving in the logical direction of getting the job done. Remember, the honeybee does not consciously realize that it is pollinating the flowers as it goes about its journey of collecting nectar to make honey.

We all remember the scene from *The Karate Kid* where the master, Mr. Miyagi, taught his student to wax the car or paint the fence in a very specific way. Even though the kid was frustrated with these seemingly pointless specificities, he did it anyway.

In the end, of course, we learn that he was practicing the essential movements of karate without even realizing he was doing it. By following Mr. Miyagi's insistent instructions, he gained a large amount of discipline and practice, and he grew the muscles that he needed to ultimately succeed in his karate tournaments.

The same principles will apply here. I'm going to have you do exercises, write things down, search for things, and even move your body.

These processes may sometimes seem disconnected from the outcomes you desire, but the reality is you will be conditioning your psychology and your body to produce results.

As your Mr. Miyagi, I ask you to commit to the following five rules as a condition of working with me.

The 5 Rules

Rule #1: Have Fun

Relax and allow yourself to have fun. This does not have to be a big, dramatic journey. As a matter of fact, it's designed to help you feel good about yourself along the way.

Yes, there will be some things that I'm gonna ask you to do that might be difficult at first. But as you're doing them, you'll find that you'll be releasing a lot of stress and a lot of pressure. You'll start to feel better.

If you come across something that you don't want to do, or it doesn't feel good when you're doing it, stop. Take a deep breath. Relax. And breathe through it. You will find that your greatest releases and paradigm shifts occur when you are able to breathe through something that feels frightening, frustrating, or uncomfortable.

Don't worry. I'm going to show you how to do that too. I will remind you how to breathe through the difficult moments as we go along.

Just remember these words: "Life is much simpler than we have been led to believe."

This is not my first rodeo. After teaching in front of over four and a half million people, I've learned a thing or two about human beings and how we function.

Rule #2: Do The Exercises

Do the exercises as prescribed. Each chapter will contain one of the five elements of Magnificence. I'm going to give you at least one exercise to complete to teach your brain and body to incorporate each element.

For each element, I'm going to give you something to write and something to search for. Understand that this process will rewire your brain.

Humans work from the top down. Your brain is the command center for everything that you do, feel, and have. It is the organ through which you process your senses and emotions and originate your actions.

There will be a desire in you to skip ahead—but don't do that! Remember to do the exercises as prescribed. They are designed the way they are for one reason: to allow you to achieve maximum results in your life.

When I suggest that you stop reading right now, put the book down, and go search for something, *do it at that moment.*

Don't hesitate, don't wait. Do it at that moment. Then pick the book back up and proceed.

Each lesson and each exercise is designed to build on the previous one, so that maximum results are produced in the end.

Personal development is *the process of* rehearsing who you wish to become. The searching process is the rewiring process, and you cannot get this process wrong unless you don't do it at all.

So do the exercises consistently and as prescribed. These exercises are not difficult, but so many of us are tempted to skip these crucial steps!

Rule #3: Keep an Open Mind

One of the biggest challenges with integrating something into one's nervous system is that often people fundamentally disagree with the advice.

Real change often feels uncomfortable and threatening. Some readers may understand the advice, and it may make sense to them at a superficial level. But deep down inside, there might be a part of them saying 'there's no way in hell I'm doing this,' or 'that's not what I believe about how this works.'

Of course, you have sought this book out because you want to grow. And I have a job in this field because I have experience in assisting the process of growth.

So I encourage you to have an open mind throughout this process. Again, keep in mind that this is not my first rodeo. Everything here is designed to build your confidence, your certainty, and your integrity.

You may find it useful to try what I call 'the Overcoat Theory.' Try this advice on. Wear it. Walk around in it for a while and see how it works with your life.

If it works for you, then keep on doing it. If you can use it to change your quality-of-life, then do it even more.

You can always take off the overcoat—or stop following the advice in this book—if it is not getting you the results you desire.

Some of the greatest lessons that I've learned in my life and the greatest changes that I've created in my life were contrary to things that I learned when I was younger.

When we are young, ideas can fall into our minds from any old source. As children we don't ask ourselves whether the person telling us "how things are" is successful or happy. We just know that they're adults, authority figures, or media sources, so they *must* be right.

As a result, we can end up with a lot of ideas that actually don't serve us very well. We may then refuse to try other ideas that contradict these "obvious facts" about the way the world works.

Human beings tend to push against what they don't agree with. We tend to move the other way without even trying on the opposing perspective.

We've all had experiences where somebody suggested something to us that we resisted and didn't do, only to discover later that we should have listened and acted upon the suggestion.

The best way to prevent that from happening is to have an open mind and consider everything. Especially when the ideas are coming from someone who already has what we want, whether that be wealth, happiness, or another form of success. Maybe, just maybe, they are a little more right about how to get that thing than the people whose ideas we internalized when we were growing up.

This real, practical, doable process has made a huge difference in the lives of millions of people around the globe. Now, it's your turn.

The question is, do you want to do it the hard way–or do you want to do it the simple way?

Rule #4: Praise

Make sure that you are praising yourself and being kind to yourself throughout this book.

I'm going to spend a whole lot of time on this in the next chapter. That's because this is the most important step toward helping you go further, faster.

One of the things that I'm going to teach you to do is to give yourself credit and acknowledge your successes each and every step of the way.

This is what drives every single thing within our nervous systems to continue to move forward.

It's the carrot we pursue each day, and it is the light at the end of the tunnel.

Rule #5: Play Full-Out

Step outside and *stay outside* of your comfort zone.

We all know that exercising to build muscle is uncomfortable. It *hurts*. This is where the common expression "no pain, no gain" used in athletic circles comes from.

Building new pathways for thought and emotion can feel similar. These processes are not usually as excruciating or taxing as exercising our muscles until we hit the point of failure, but they are usually not as easy as sitting on the couch watching TV either.

After all, if they were that easy, they wouldn't do anything for us.

When we engage ourselves fully and do things that are not initially comfortable, we grow in skill and intelligence. In fact, when we step outside of our comfort zone, what we are really doing is *expanding* our comfort zone.

In time, with practice, growth will occur such that something we were previously unable to do becomes comfortable. Just as an athlete gains the ability to complete astounding feats of athletic prowess, we can add to our abilities any skill, ability, or emotion we please with persistent and sometimes uncomfortable practice.

As long as you are going to do this, you might as well do it full-out. If you're going to get uncomfortable, you may as well throw yourself into the exercise entirely so that you will reap the maximum gains in the minimum amount of time.

Since the human nervous system is designed to move away from pain and towards pleasure, we often avoid doing things we are not comfortable with. These negative responses surface in any number of behaviors like procrastination, lack of interest, hesitation, neglect, fear of failure, uncertainty, self-doubt, and denial.

Keep an eye out for the following signs that you are experiencing discomfort:

"I can't do this. There's no point in trying."
"This is too hard. I can't do it."
"This isn't going to work. It's poppycock!"

"I'll never be that *person."*

Remember, these thoughts and feelings are not true statements. They are beliefs that arise when we start to become uncomfortable. Just as an athlete can gain new abilities by pushing through physical discomfort, we can accomplish anything we set our minds to by breathing through this mental and emotional discomfort to reach the other side.

In fact, we *must* do this in order to reach some of our goals!

We'll be eliminating these and other negative thoughts and behaviors that slow us down as we move through this book. We'll replace them with behaviors that will be fruitful and successful because you deserve to see and feel how you can function at your optimum level.

If and when this process feels uncomfortable and even hard, this is the time to dig in and realize that success is right around the corner.

Keep in mind that there are no wrong answers here. This is not an IQ test. It's not a contest or a test of your abilities. The whole point of this process is to demonstrate that your beliefs about your abilities and limitations may not be correct.

The only way you can get this process wrong is to not follow the steps at all.

You'll find that a large number of the questions that I ask you are personal to you. What is true to you might not be the same for other people.

The purpose of these questions, again, is not for you to give "the right answer." *It is for you to discover the answers that lie within you.* No two great people in the world are alike. Every one of them has a combination of desires, skills, and predispositions that allows them to contribute something totally unique to the world.

Ideas about how you "should" answer these questions are counterproductive because they limit you in discovering your true Magnificence.

So *don't* allow yourself to get caught up in the web of guessing what other people think, or guessing what the "right" answer might be to a question that I've asked. These questions are not designed to have "right" answers, but to get at the *truth* at the heart of you.

Just let the answers flow from your heart and you'll do just fine.

One of the greatest gifts that you're going to give yourself is the gift of self-appreciation. That's what we're going to do here: get to know ourselves, and then *appreciate* ourselves.

Terminology

Statistically one person only understands exactly what another person means about 7% of the time. If I say the word "car" to you, you might think of a Volkswagen or a Mercedes-Benz. On the other hand, I might be thinking about a Ford F150, a clown car, or maybe even a 1938 Plymouth business coupe.

To avoid confusion and make sure that we're on the same page, I want to give you some terminology so that you'll know exactly what I mean when I say certain things. Otherwise you won't have a reference for them and you'll have to guess at my true meaning. Some of these may be words or phrases that you've never heard before, or you've never heard them used in this specific context.

We've all had situations where we've heard somebody use a word that we've never heard before and we don't have a reference for. Sometimes people feel intimidated or challenged by not knowing. Sometimes people will shut down and not ask what that word means because they are afraid of appearing stupid or ignorant. The problem with that strategy is that this is how you get left behind.

Many leaders know that there truly *is* no such thing as a "stupid question." Often, asking seemingly simple or obvious questions can yield surprising truths.

To give us a jump-start on revealing these truths, I like to teach in a way that preemptively answers these simple questions. I like to explain ahead of time what something means. I like to teach to what I call the "lowest common denominator," or LCD.

The LCD does not represent people who are less intelligent: it represents the way in which we can all understand a concept, regardless of what specialized background knowledge, experiences, and learning styles we may have.

One of my great mentors used to tell me that if you can't explain something to a third grader, then you don't understand it yourself. If your attempted explanation goes over the heads of most people, then your understanding of the topic is not as deep or effective as it could be.

This same mentor also used to say: "Learn it until you can teach it, and then teach it."

It's when you fully understand a subject that you'll be able to help others who have different learning strategies than you do. That's when you really know that you understand something inside and out.

That's why I sometimes say something, and then say it again, and then say it again another way to make sure that everybody gets it. This is how I practice the LCD. In the process I am not only doing my best to ensure that everyone is on the same page; I am also *reinforcing* these simple concepts which change our thoughts and emotions through *practice*. Thereby I grow myself, and each and every student.

So if you find yourself getting frustrated because you've heard something once before, stop and ask yourself a few questions:

Am I gaining something from this repetition?

Can I teach it in a way that others will understand it?

Am I actually practicing what I know?

To know something is one thing. To practice it, do it, and get results is another thing. Talk is cheap. Activity and results are what really matter. And repetition in this work, just like in physical exercise, always increases the strength of our thoughts, emotions, and actions.

The following are some of the terms and phrases that you will encounter on this journey. There's no need to memorize them. Just read through them. When you come across them again, if you aren't sure you understand them, you can always come back to this section as a reference guide.

Pro Sequences

The first term I will use throughout this process is '*pro sequences.*' These are the opposite of '*consequences.*'

Consequences are often viewed as unfavorable results of wrong actions. *Pro sequences* are the opposite.

Pro sequences are the wonderful, great, and fortunate events that happen as a result of the premeditated and deliberate activities that you establish to align with your goals.

This term gives you something to look forward to. You now know that you *will* experience favorable results from the actions you undertake during this process. Wait until you begin to experience these in your life!

Contrived Human Nature

Contrived human nature is another important term to understand as you proceed through the journey to Magnificence.

When we come kicking and screaming into this life, we know only a very few things instinctively. We know we need to eat, drink, and sleep. We feel this in our bones. We know how to squirm and cry out when we are uncomfortable.

For the most part, we have to learn everything else.

Those instinctive behaviors and feelings we are born with can be described as human nature. They are for the most part automatic and we don't have to think about them to execute them.

Contrived human nature refers to the actions, feelings, and ideas that we *learn* from others growing up. *Contrived human nature* is the deliberate learning of behavior and emotion until it becomes a natural/automatic extension of our lives.

Many of us may not realize that our *contrived human nature* is learned. What we learn in childhood often becomes our default. It is "just the way things are" or "just the way we are." We may never have had much exposure to a different way of doing things.

Much of what we learn is picked up from the social and cultural context in which we are raised. This means that a great deal of what we absorb is gleaned without ever questioning the value or efficacy of these ideas about "the way things are."

The elements of Magnificence allow you to question *contrived human nature* and see if these ideas really hold value in helping you achieve your goals. More than that, recognizing that much of our human nature is learned, or 'contrived,' allows us to *change our nature* if we want to. It gives us the framework necessary to question and reshape much of what we may currently think of as "just the way things are."

Psychology

Psychology, as I use the term here, refers to nothing more than your *consistent mindset*.

Said differently, the thoughts that you think over and over again are your psychology.

Change your consistent thoughts, and your life will change forever.

Your psychology is where you are now mentally. Tuning into your current mindset will help you determine where you were in the past, where you are now, how this differs from where you want to be, and the steps you need to take to get to where you want to be.

'Courage' vs. 'Bravery'

While courage and bravery may seem synonymous, I'd like to differentiate them for the purposes of Magnificence training.

Bravery is *temporary*. I can bravely take an injection that I know will make me better even though I hate needles.

However, courage is an *element of the spirit*. It's profoundly deeper and more potent than mere bravery.

Courage motivates us, moves us, and grounds us in our beliefs and actions.

No one can give it to you: you must build it yourself. And it is one of your most powerful allies in your Magnificence transformation.

Discipline

'Discipline' is a term with which we are very familiar. Generally, it is infused with negative connotations. Many people try to teach discipline using punishment or negative reinforcement. This has the unfortunate side effect of causing many of us to be wary of the very idea of 'discipline.'

Let's redefine the word and give it a much more positive connotation. In Magnificence training, 'discipline' simply means doing.

Discipline is doing the prescribed activity or application no matter what, even (and especially) when it's difficult or when it's inconvenient. Since these activities will yield great results in our lives, in this book discipline will be taught through *positive* reinforcements and rewards.

Discipline is simply the act of doing something *consistently*.

Rather than looking at discipline in an unfavorable light, recognize that you *already have it* when you are doing the things that you like. All we are going to do is transfer that trait to the things that you don't yet have the experience to *know* that you like.

Try shifting your focus to treat those rare times as golden opportunities for overcoming old, bad habits. When you perform an action prescribed in this book, even if it feels uncomfortable at the time, trust that it *will* yield great rewards and positive reinforcement once you have some experience with it.

(Don't worry. I'm going to show you how to do that too).

Redefining roadblocks as opportunities will forever change the landscape of your Magnificence journey.

'Coach' vs. 'Mentor'

The concepts of 'coach' vs. 'mentor' require some explanation and clarification because people so often view the two words as interchangeable. However, there is a difference.

'Coaching' requires a higher level of understanding and insight about human performance, but this does not presuppose that a coach be better at what they're coaching than you are. The coach's skills lie in helping people to grow and perform; *not* necessarily in performing the specific action that they're coaching.

Michael Jordan and Tiger Woods both have coaches who are essential to helping them master their games; however, Michael Jordan is obviously a better basketball player than any of his coaches.

The role of coaching is to offer insight, examine a person's performance, and recommend strategies that will help them to perform better.

A mentor, on the other hand, is someone who excels at your specific craft, and who provides the insight of a coach as well as the benefit of a great deal of experience with your specific skill.

I will act as your mentor through this journey to Magnificence, guiding you through to a performance level that I have already mastered.

'Practice' vs. 'Rehearsal'

We have all heard the old cliché: "Practice makes perfect."

There's another, more powerful version: "*Perfect* practice makes perfect."

Here, the word 'practice' just means doing something over and over again—like going through scales on the piano for hours on end. It may work, but it's not the most effective strategy, or even the most fun or pleasant.

The best strategy for any level of repetition is to practice with purpose—to *rehearse.*

'Practice' is simply the performance of an action. 'Rehearsal' is practicing *for a specific future performance.*

The concept of 'practice' vs. 'rehearsal' highlights the importance of how you approach practice—you treat it like it matters.

Rehearsal is not simply a repetitive act that you engage in. Powerful rehearsal puts you center stage as if it's time to perform.

The pressure is on. This is the moment. Your central nervous system is alive, and it's time for you to perform.

You can see, then, how a 'rehearsal' differs from the idea of merely repeating an action, and how approaching repetition with an attitude of *rehearsing* for the future will help you achieve faster results.

'Inspiration' vs. 'Empowerment'

At one time or another, we have all *felt* inspired. The important distinction to make here is that inspiration is a *feeling*. This feeling generally results from seeing someone else perform at a high level that we hope to emulate, or from hearing or reading content that we hope to apply in order to gain similar results.

Empowerment is more than a feeling.

To be empowered is to be armed with the tools, the desire, and the ability to effect change.

While feelings are powerful motivators, empowerment moves us past motivation. Empowerment includes the acquisition of the necessary *skills* for success, including the *implementation* of those skills into *action* that produces *change* in your life.

Creality

This term cannot be found in a dictionary. I ran into this concept decades ago, and I loved it so much I started using it.

The theory behind the concept of *creality* is simple: *we create our own reality.*

When I first heard the words, "as we think, so we are," it was like a lightbulb went on inside me. I learned that whatever we imagine or think about in any given moment, we feel. And subsequently, we react and behave according to the meaning we gave to that thought.

I'll give you some examples:

If you imagine licking a lemon, your mouth will water.

If you think about your lover cheating on you, your heart will race, your blood pressure will rise, and you may feel angry and/or jealous. You may lash out at someone or cry or behave in any number of ways.

Our thoughts *literally* change the biochemical messengers that our brain sends throughout our bodies.

The blood that courses through your veins when you are thinking about something happy is different from the blood that courses through your veins when you think sad thoughts.

In the moment of any thought, we actually *feel*—and on some level *believe*—that it is reality.

This is an idea that seems so simple it can easily be dismissed. However, the truth of the concept cannot be so easily swept aside.

Steve Jobs had an idea—one that, at the time, had no basis in any reality. From that idea, Apple's Macintosh computer was born.

The word *creality* is just crazy enough to remind us how critical it is to embrace our own crazy ideas of the reality that we want to create.

The only true folly lies in tossing aside our Magnificent ideas, our breathtaking dreams, and our life-changing visions because we don't believe in ourselves enough to reach for the branch with the highest fruit.

Creality is the ladder to the good stuff. Don't fear the climb.

Concentration

This is a technique that should never be underestimated.

Concentration painted the ceiling of the Sistine Chapel. Concentration calls for bringing everything you have to the game.

When your mental, physical, spiritual, and verbal acuities join together to work in concert to solve problems or search for strategies—you are *unstoppable*. Your brain is its own Magnificent computer, and when you harness its computing power and apply it toward the achievement of a goal, magic happens.

Skill

Lastly, I'd like to clarify the use of the word 'skill.' For our purposes, 'skill' comprises the ability to reproduce an activity consistently, producing the same or enhanced results with each repetition.

Remember that all skills are learned, and all skills can be improved through practice and rehearsal. We can all become better at anything quickly.

Most of us take for granted the fact that we are highly skilled at countless things already because of social influence, media, and our own lack of appreciation of ourselves. We forget that at one time we couldn't walk, talk, or tie our shoes. We weren't born knowing how to do any one of those literally hundreds of thousands of things we no longer have to think about as we do them.

And we do these things extremely well—*every time*. Things that were once difficult and seemingly impossible to you are now done with unconscious ease and flawless expertise.

You are in fact *awesome* at thousands of things.

The good news is that you have acquired skills before So we can say with confidence that you can and will do it again.

If you could learn to do all the things you *already* do on a daily basis, you can learn to do *anything* with sufficient discipline and rehearsal.

Your First Assignment

I need to ask you two questions, and I need you to answer these right now.

Later, I'm going to ask you these questions again. When I do, most of you will find that your answers have changed.

So, as you answer these questions, pay attention to what you are focusing on to find your answers. Pay attention to what this process *feels* like, and what truths you *feel* when answering.

Are you ready?

Question #1: What Do You Want?

What do you want?

What are you hoping this book and this information will give you?

When you have finished reading and doing the exercises, what changes do you want to have experienced?

What do you hope to have in your possession at the end of this process?

Why did you pick up this book? Why did you commit to spending your time, energy, and capital towards this goal?

Maybe you're discouraged about your business, a relationship, your physique, or the way things are headed in your life. Perhaps you've been in a rut and you're not feeling so happy right now. Or maybe you're generally fulfilled, you're healthy, happy, and wealthy beyond your wildest dreams, but you're missing that take-no-prisoners kind of joy that allows you to recognize that anything is possible!

Maybe you're satisfied and happy as a box full of French Bulldog puppies on a summer day, and you just want to learn how to maximize this, or sustain it, or pass it on to others.

No matter what your answer is, you came to the right place.

Write your answers in a journal or in the space below.

If you don't want to write in the space provided in this book, then be sure to get yourself a nice notebook.

It is critical that you do the writing exercises, and that you *value* them. Give yourself the time and space in which to complete them because they are a big part of your growth process.

What do you want? Why did you pick up this book?

_____

_____

Question #2: How Will You Feel When You Have It?

How will you feel when you have what you want?

What will you do with your newfound bounty?

Will you feel relieved and satisfied? Will you be excited and motivated?

What will you do? Who will you help? What will you build, etc.?

_____

_____

_____

_____

_____

_____

_____

_____

_____

_____

_____

_____

If you're like most people, you're guessing at these answers right now. You may not have been invited to deeply consider these questions *ever*, or in a very long time. We are rarely encouraged to consider our wildest dreams and what it would feel like to realize them.

You'll get the opportunity to answer these questions again later in the book. You will get to see how the answers change as you perform these exercises, which will expand your range of beliefs and feelings about what is possible.

But for now, I want you to search your brain to answer these questions. Answer them thoroughly and take time to see how these answers *feel*.

The process of growth starts right now.

CHAPTER 2

The First Element:
Integrity

"The measure of a man is not what he says he'll do or what he does. The measure of a man is what he does when nobody's looking. It's what he does when he doesn't have to do it."

— Les Brown

In 1959, my father and his four friends were on their way home from work when they decided to stop at a restaurant for a bite to eat.

All five of them were flight line mechanics at Grand Forks Air Force Base in North Dakota. They walked into the restaurant and sat down at an empty table. They were immediately approached by the manager and owner. My father and two of the other men were refused service and told to leave.

You see, the two men who were allowed to stay were white and my father and his two friends were black. In solidarity, all five of them left the restaurant.

Things were quite different back then. The nation was going through some serious growing pains, and it was not uncommon for black people to be refused service. It was especially degrading for my father because all of the men were serving their country as Airmen. This service apparently did not mean much to this restaurant manager because of the color of their skin.

Even though it was extremely unpopular and downright dangerous in those days, my father chose to step up and bring the matter to the attention of the police and the courts. He wanted to stop the same thing from happening to future generations of black people.

The case became well-known in that area. When I was older, my father showed me pictures and articles in the newspaper about the court battle. In the end, my father won the case. As a result, a law was changed: it became illegal to refuse service to someone in Grand Forks because of the color of their skin.

He didn't have to do this. If he had not filed the suit, no one would have known or blamed him for it. And in many ways, this action could have cost him dearly. Filing a lawsuit is not easy. That's why not many people do it, and those who do are often hailed as heroes.

Any ordinary citizen who has filed a lawsuit over discrimination or injustice knows that it is an extremely stressful and often frightening process. The plaintiff often faces public scrutiny, and opposition lawyers may threaten dire consequences for the plaintiff, their family, and their career in an effort to get them to drop the case.

But my father felt in his heart it was the right thing to do. He believed that all people deserve the same rights and he believed that somebody needed to stand up and do the right thing. This was who he was, so that's what he did.

He believed in himself, he believed in other people and mankind. He believed that the world was a good place and justice would prevail.

His actions were congruent with his beliefs. The way he felt was integrated into the way that he behaved. He believed that a person has to stand for something. He believed that if you don't, you'll fall for anything. He believed that talk was cheap and actions spoke louder than words. He truly lived his life with integrity.

The word integrity comes from the root word "integrate." This means that two or more components are joined together to create a new, more powerful and significant idea, device, or entity.

In the work of Magnificence, we mix together the essences of five standards to create one congruent standard. But true integrity means that these standards *remain* together and create a whole which does not bend or break with the tides of popularity, convenience, and other outside factors.

Integrity also has another meaning: the solidness, or intactness, of a structure. A structure that has integrity can stand against any outside force, just as my father did.

Human Integrity is when the beliefs that you hold about yourself, other people, and the world around you are integrated into your consistent behaviors and actions.

Your beliefs are your own personal truth. Your true beliefs are found not just in the words you speak, but in the behaviors you put out into the world.

Two Types of Integrity: Inner and Outer

Inner integrity is when your actions are congruent with your beliefs and values. When your actions, activities, and behavior reflect what you believe to be true, then you are congruent and have integrity.

When you have inner integrity, you actually feel it in your being. It shows up in the work that you do and the results that you produce.

Whether we are aware of it or not, we all have and demonstrate inner integrity. All of our actions are rooted in our beliefs. It's unconscious in nature and we rarely think about it before we act.

It's a feeling that comes about in milliseconds. So fast that we don't notice that we have made a decision to react or respond to a situation or circumstance.

The question we now face is this: *Is our integrity what we want it to be?* Are the beliefs and values we consistently act on the beliefs and values we wish to hold, create, and show to the world? Or do our actions show values and beliefs that we do *not* wish to have and which we may wish to change?

Outer integrity is when our actions and behaviors match the words that we speak.

If you tell someone that you're going to show up somewhere on time and your inner beliefs say that you are an on-time person and can be counted on and trusted, then you will probably show up on time and maybe even a few minutes early.

You have outer integrity because you're doing what you said you're going to do. Your actions have matched your words and beliefs.

If, on the other hand, you tell someone that you're gonna show up on time but deep inside you know that you're always late for things or you feel that you are not *capable* of showing up on time, then the likelihood of you showing up on time is in the toilet. You actually believe that showing up late is part of who you are and that's why it's repeated over and over again in your life.

Now you are out of integrity because you're not doing what you said you were going to do. What you have said and what you truly believe about yourself do not match up. You're out of integrity.

This scenario plays out over and over in many people's lives in the form of procrastination. Deep inside we all *want* to do what we commit to do, but there's something deeper which tells us that something is wrong and that we're not capable or responsible or willing to do the task at hand.

A great example is dieting. Many people want to lose weight. When they feel bad about themselves and are motivated, they commit to starting a diet, joining a gym, or working out. They will tell their friends what they want to do, but when it comes down to actually doing it they fall short and don't because they don't believe that they can.

Then they create excuses justifying why it's okay that they didn't meet their own desires. They say that they didn't want to do it, or they believe that they'll do it later, or that they just couldn't do it because of some outside circumstances. As long as they believe these excuses, it will be easy for outside forces to get in their way in the future.

Because they committed to doing it out loud and then did not complete the action, they are now out of integrity with their words. They are, however, in integrity with their beliefs about themselves. This is a vicious circle and it drives people crazy, even to the point of depression, because they can't understand why they're not doing what they commit to doing.

The same could just as easily apply to any goal. The same sequence of events is involved in concluding that we "can't" reach any goal we can conceive of.

Of the two types of integrity, inner integrity is the most important and most powerful. It is your internal beliefs and feelings which will determine whether you have outer integrity or not. This is why, in this book, we will focus on your thoughts and feelings before we expect to see real changes to your behavior.

When something is said to have structural integrity, it means that the components that make up that particular object are not only strong on their own: the manner in which they are linked together creates that object's overall strength.

Integrity is the first and most critical element for anybody who wants to achieve their dreams, goals, and desires in a major way. It's an absolute must if you want to go further, faster.

Integrity dictates the actions that you will and will not take. As you go for your dreams, goals, and desires, I encourage you to live and move forward with a sense of integrity.

Examine your thoughts and feelings. What do you really feel and believe? Are these the things that you *want* to feel and believe? Are they the things which will lead to the actions you want to see in your life?

If not, take time to explore new feelings and beliefs. Feel how your mind and body change as you explore these new pathways. Next time you get up to act and really do something, will your action now be more consistent with what you would *like* your actions to be?

Galvanize your actions to match your core beliefs, and you will find that the universe stands up and takes notice.

Show me any great person and I guarantee you that at their core they are congruent with their beliefs about themselves, about other people, and about the world around them.

But don't get it twisted. It works both ways. Your brain on its own can't tell whether something is good or true or not. It will believe whatever you tell it and act accordingly. If you truly believe something, your mind and your body will not question it.

You will just carry out its prime directive as though it were real and true.

There have been many men with sinister and destructive beliefs who acted upon those beliefs and brought harm to themselves and others. These cases could have been changed or prevented if they had more critically examined their beliefs and feelings.

It doesn't much matter what you say. It only matters what you believe, for your beliefs drive your actions.

Remember: any belief is just a feeling of absolute certainty about something. Our beliefs are supported by the things that we've experienced in the past.

You believe that you can drive a car because you've done it before. And as a result, you don't question it. You just get behind the wheel and you drive without hesitation. Your actions are in alignment with your beliefs about yourself and about driving a car.

If you are not in line with your beliefs, you will sabotage yourself. You will procrastinate and hesitate. And worst of all, you will drive yourself crazy trying to figure out why you can't seem to get ahead.

If you believe that you are not smart enough or that you are too unlucky or that you are unworthy of love, then you will behave as though you don't deserve good things. You will shy away from opportunities. You will tell yourself you don't have the skills or comfort level to take advantage of them. You will give in to temptations and distractions that derail your success.

But if you have self-love and believe that you are a good person, if you believe that you deserve the best and you add value to others' lives, your confidence will soar. Your self-esteem will blossom and you will take more action towards your goals. You will also feel good doing it. You will have more drive and pull, more energy, and be more willing to step up and do more.

If you believe that other people are judging you, or that they somehow have some malice against you, then you will treat them differently and you will behave accordingly. They may not think or feel that way at all, but if you believe they do then you will behave in a way that may indeed alienate you from them.

On the other hand, if you truly believe that someone loves you and respects you, then you will feel differently. You will feel loved and supported, and you will be more apt to do things that are positive and enthusiastic in terms of creating and accomplishing. If you feel that people like you, respect you, and even adore you, then you will have less anxiety about speaking up, asking for help, and leading others.

If you believe that the world is a cruel and unjust place or that things happen for no reason and that bad things always happen to you, you will shy away from opportunities, make excuses, procrastinate and hesitate. You'll do this because you fear the worst instead of having confidence and joy in the best.

If you believe that the world around you is full of opportunities, that situations and circumstances are put on your path to serve as opportunities for you to grow, then you will take more chances. You will step up more often and, as a result, you will create more abundance.

We have so many beliefs that it is impossible to name them all. It is impossible to be aware of them all. And here's the clincher—most of us don't even know what we believe, or where those beliefs came from.

You would drive yourself crazy if you tried to figure out what all your beliefs are and where they came from. But upon closer look, you'll recognize that all of your activities are, on some level, in accordance with what you believe.

The good news is that you don't have to know what all of your beliefs are, or where they came from, in order to change them to suit your dreams, goals, and desires. All you have to do is start introducing new beliefs and these will automatically overwrite the old ones.

So rather than try to figure out what all of your beliefs are, let's work on clearing a space to place the most empowering and significant beliefs into your nervous system. Once that is done, you will be able to respond with actions that support those beliefs.

Said differently, we can create a set of beliefs that cause you to react and respond with favorable actions. That is, the actions that are needed to bring your dreams and goals to fruition.

Integrity Exercise: Part One

Let's explore your core beliefs about yourself—past, present, and future.

Look back on your life. If you were to describe yourself as a child from the ages of five years old to 15 years old, how would you describe yourself?

Don't worry. Nobody's gonna see this but you. Be bluntly honest with yourself.

At those ages, were you happy? Did you believe that you were a good person and deserved the best? Did you believe that you were likable and strong?

Or did you believe that there was something wrong with you? That you were flawed and somehow not worthy?

Think about how you felt about yourself back then. Were you a confident child? Were you scared?

Were you outgoing and fun and engaging? Or were you introverted and shy? Did you take chances and risks? Did you easily follow others, or were you a leader?

There's no right or wrong answer here. All there is is *information*. The point is to stir up your memories and cause your brain to search. You're going to find some pretty interesting things as you dig deep and remember some of the things that you thought about, believed, and felt. If this is difficult for you, you can do it a little bit at a time in chunks.

Either way, it's incredibly important that you do this exercise. Most people never, in their entire lives, will do anything like this exercise. This is what is going to set you apart from most people. This is what's going to help you grow.

Don't try and second guess what we're going to do with this, or what any of this means right now. *Just do the exercise.* Let your brain run free. Remember who you were, how you felt, what you thought, and what you believed about yourself.

Lastly, give yourself a name. It can be your own name, but if you had a nickname for yourself as a child what would it have been? And if you didn't, what is the nickname that you would give yourself now as that child?

Take all the time you need to answer this question:

I (Insert your full name here) believed that I was…

_____

_____

_____

_____

_____

_____

_____

_____

_____

_____

_____

_____

_____

Integrity Exercise: Part Two

Now, it's time to discover who you are now. What do you believe about yourself right now? Write down the good, the bad, and the otherwise. Use the same criteria as we did on the previous exercise.

Do you believe to your core that you're a good person? Do you believe that you're flawed or there's something wrong with you? Do you believe that you deserve the best? Or do you believe that you are somehow cursed, and you don't deserve to have the things that others do?

Dig deep and come up with other things that you believe about yourself.

Remember most people will never dig this deep. Because you are here and willing to do the work, you will benefit from it. I promise you that on the other side of this, you're going to be thankful that you did this.

It is well worth spending this time right now so that you can build the type of identity that serves you and your future.

I (Insert your full name here) believe that I am…

_____

_____

_____

_____

_____

_____

_____

Integrity Exercise: Part Three

Now it's time to have some fun. It's time to be creative and use your imagination.

One of my great mentors once taught me that the best way to predict the future is to imagine it. This is a place where most people fall short. Because of their beliefs about themselves, they are afraid to really dream and imagine their dreams coming true. Deep down inside, they don't feel like they deserve them or are able to achieve them.

Now it's time to be selfish in a good way.

As you imagine yourself in the future–maybe five years from now–what do you want to believe about yourself at that time? What would be the best things that you would love to have as part of your core belief system?

Do you want to believe that you are the best and worthy of the best? Do you want to believe that you are fundamentally a happy person?

As a tip, think of somebody that you admire. Think of somebody that you have a lot of respect for and hold in high esteem. Now, think of the way they carry themselves. What do you imagine they think of themselves?

Think of somebody who has confidence without arrogance. Somebody that has certainty and pride and a level of centeredness that you would love to have for yourself. What beliefs do you think they have about themselves?

Remember, you're making this stuff up. So as long as you're making it up, you might as well make up good stuff.

If you're fortunate enough to know somebody like this and you have access to them, you might ask them what they believe about themselves.

Remember, we can borrow other people's beliefs or make our own up from scratch. So have fun with this one.

In the future, I (Insert your full name here) believe that I am…

_____

_____

_____

_____

_____

_____

_____

_____

_____

_____

_____

_____

_____

_____

CHAPTER 3

The Amazing Human Machine
Or, How We Function

"I stand in awe of my body."
— Henry David Thoreau

*"Take care of your body. It's the only place
you have to live."*
— Jim Rohn

Everybody is great at something. It's been my experience in life that everybody can teach me something, because everybody can do something better than I can.

You may have a special talent for playing music, riding a bicycle, riding a horse, or playing a game. The sky's the limit, and I believe that everybody can teach me something.

Having said that, I must point out that the things that you're the best at are the things that you have spent the most time learning, studying, practicing, and experiencing. They aren't things you're born knowing how to do; they're things you set out to learn.

I happen to be good at studying human behavior. From an early age, I've been fascinated by human beings and what makes us tick. What makes us do what we do? What makes us move forward or backward? All of the intricacies of how we function fascinate me.

I could sit and talk for hours and hours about all of the different intricacies of human beings, from the makeup of our cells, to our muscles, to how we think, what we do, and how we feel. I could write a whole other book on that.

To serve you best and to best produce the outcomes that you want to create in your life, I'm going to simplify it. I'm going to break it down to the Lowest Common Denominator so that we all understand it thoroughly.

I'm going to show you the fundamentals of how you function as a human being. Once you understand that, then we can use that information to get the very best out of ourselves.

More specifically, we can use this knowledge to learn how to embed the five elements of greatness deep into our nervous system so that they become a natural extension of who we are. We can turn these elements into our "defaults," the ways we behave automatically, instead of having to put forth effort to summon up these elements every time they are called for.

Now, this is going to be super, super, super simple. But remember, it's the simple things that make the most sense. It's the simple things that people will actually *do*, thereby getting results.

It's important that you have an open mind and just allow yourself to live in this possibility that things can be this simple.

Let's see how powerful a simple idea can be.

The Top-Down Theory

Here it is…

Think, Feel, Do, Have.

That is the syntax of how we function as human beings. To get the most out of this book, this is one of the biggest things you need to understand.

If you get it, then you'll understand how to cause a chain reaction that will produce your desired results. So here's your first assignment.

Memorize this saying:

As I think,
So I feel,
As I feel,
So I do,
As I do,
So I have.

Say it over and over and over again until you don't have to read it. Lock it into your memory. As you repeat it, you are creating new pathways in your brain.

Remember, everything that we're doing is designed to produce results. This sequence will become a deep-seated understanding of who you are, and what makes you do what you do.

More specifically when you find yourself doing something, you will be able to go back and figure out *why* you're doing what you're doing. You will be able to change and edit—or reinforce and strengthen—the cause of your action from the top down.

Think of it like this: your brain is the command center of the rest of your body. Your eyes, nose, ears, and tongue are all on your head. This is not by mistake: it's by design. All of them are input portals to your brain.

When you see something, your eyes send a signal to your brain. When you hear something, your ears send a signal to your brain. When you smell something or taste something, those signals go directly to your brain. All the information from all the nerves in your body consolidate in your spinal cord, through which they transmit information directly into your brain.

Your brain has two jobs. and two jobs only:

1. Interpret the input, and
2. Decide the appropriate output to send to the rest of your body.

We call that the process of *thinking*. The thinking process is just your brain making pictures and words.

And here's the clincher: it never stops. Your brain never stops thinking. It never stops making pictures and words—even when you're sleeping. It *especially* doesn't stop making pictures and words when you're asleep. You might not always *remember* your dreams, because the part of your brain that forms memories switches off during sleep. But your brain is always making up pictures and words.

From those pictures and words, your brain tells the rest of your body what to do. Obviously, there are a lot of details to this thinking process, but for the most part we don't need to understand these.

All we have to understand is that constant evaluation of input and generation of output signals to the rest of your body is the main function of the brain.

Keeping that in mind (no pun intended), if the brain and the thinking process is the command center, that's the place to go if we want to make a change in the simplest, most powerful and long-lasting way.

One of the first signals that your brain sends goes to your heart. When something dangerous happens, your brain sends signals to your heart to beat faster, produce more blood pressure, and activate several other things in sequence. Different sequences can produce different emotions.

Some of you may notice that when you are feeling an emotion, you feel it at different places in your body. Many strong emotions include a rapid or pounding heartbeat.

Your heart is telling you how to feel at any given moment. If your brain says what's going on around you is happy, light, and joyful then your heart will be happy, light, and joyful. If your brain interprets the thoughts it is receiving as being concerned, doubtful or uncertain then you will in turn feel those emotions.

Your brain is telling you how to feel at all times. This happens unconsciously most of the time. You may not realize it's happening all the time—you may not even be conscious of how you feel all the time. Have you ever stopped and realized suddenly how stressed, fearful, or excited you were?

But even if you weren't conscious of these emotions, I guarantee they were determining your actions. You may have even noticed them because you did something that surprised you.

Whatever you do or don't do is a result of how you feel. Regardless of the logic or the facts, your emotions override and even command your actions.

Whichever emotions are strongest in any given moment will always dominate your thoughts and actions.

Part of a person may feel like they want to go to the gym, work out, lose some weight, and get healthy. But if a larger part of their brain is saying 'that's going to be painful,' 'I don't want to do that,' and 'I don't feel like doing that,' then those will be the stronger signals going to your heart. After weighing its input from your brain, your heart is going to say, 'screw it, let's eat cake.'

The trick to creating change is to tell that brain of yours what to think. More specifically, to tell that brain of yours *how* to think about certain things and *which* things to think. When you do this, that brain of yours will start sending signals to your heart to make it feel better about whatever you *want* to feel better about.

That's why we say, 'as we think, so we feel.'

Now let's talk about our actions. What will we actually do?

Remember, it's not what you think or feel that produces results. It's what you *do* that creates real change and ultimately results. What we think and feel are useful tools to change our actions, but the actions are the only things that really count. If what we're thinking and feeling is not creating the actions we desire, then we've missed something important in choosing our thoughts and feelings!

Remember that knowledge is not power. Knowledge is actually just stored information. Every single one of us has a surplus of information. Whether we are using the information that is helpful to us to inform our thoughts, feelings, and actions is the real question.

Remember this. Everything that you've ever touched, tasted, smelled, heard, or felt is stored somewhere in your brain. Those experiences are locked away in your brain's file cabinets, and your brain uses them as references to draw conclusions while it is interpreting input. Based on that input, it tells your body how to feel and what chemicals to release to cause your muscles to move or not to move.

Because knowledge is not power and knowledge has to be accessed through the thinking process, we have to ask ourselves: 'What is power? What is it that produces results?'

The answer is *activity*. Not action... *Activity*.

It's critical that you understand the difference between action and activity, because it's the 'activity' part that is the deciding factor as to how your life is going to be.

Action is temporary. Action is doing something once or twice or maybe several times towards a specific goal or outcome. Many of us have started something with the best of intentions, but somewhere along the way stopped doing it.

The physical fitness industry is constantly booming because at the very beginning of the year thousands and thousands of people buy gym memberships with the best of intentions to show up and work out. But the amount of people who actually show up after just a few weeks is staggeringly low— about 3 to 5%.

Upon further investigation, studies show that the reason people don't keep going back is that it's difficult and painful. And going to the gym once or twice doesn't produce instant, noticeable results right away. So, most people quit after just one or two sessions, and, in the end, they're not going to get *any* results because they have stopped undertaking the action.

Activity, on the other hand, is an action repeated consistently, over and over and over and over again, until you surpass your goal. That means that performing this action once or twice or maybe even 10 times may get you some results, but continuing to do it consistently over a *long* period of time is what's going to produce the best results.

The way you feel is responsible for creating persistent activity over time.

Do you feel empowered when you feel excited? If you feel enthusiastic and called towards your outcome, then that feeling will override feelings of pain and discomfort. So obviously, the trick is to get your brain to send your heart and body signals that say 'feel good about going to the gym and working out!'

I'm going to show you different ways to make that happen, but it's important to all of them that you understand this thinking → feeling → doing → having sequence.

The results that you get in your life come from the action and activities that you've performed. Going back to losing weight.

Developing a better body. Truly excelling in your career or craft. Having spectacular relationships.

All those things are only going to happen as a result of the consistent actions that you take continuously.

This is the law. This is how we function as human beings.

As you think,
So you feel,
As you feel,
So you do,
As you do,
So you create and have.

That's it. That's all you need to know about you and how you function.

Now, let's get to work.

Through the rest of this process, you will be discovering your own thought process, your own belief systems, and your own virtues as well as creating new ones that serve you and your higher purpose.

CHAPTER 4

The Second Element:
Tenacity

"To succeed in life in today's world, you must have the will and tenacity to finish the job."
— Chin-Ning Chu

"Tenacity is when you follow your heart when the whole world is screaming to get back into your head."
— Sonia Choquette

"My strength lies solely in my tenacity."
— Louis Pasteur

Life does not belong to those who start things. Life belongs to those who finish things.

There's something about tenacity. If you're serious about your goals and dreams, achieving them requires tenacity. My father had this simple rule:

WHATEVER YOUR START, YOU FINISH.

He used to say: "The *try place* is down the street on somebody else's doorstep. This is the *DO place*. In this house, we get things done."

He believed that when you start something, you finish it.

Life does not belong to those who start things. Life belongs to those who finish things. And he had tenacity and determination to see it through.

My father's word was his bond. As we look at ourselves and we look at our goals and dreams, tenacity goes hand-in-hand with integrity. We want to be in alignment with the things that we say.

It's one thing to say: "Practice what you preach." It's another to *preach* what you *practice*.

And that's what my father did. He was in alignment with his beliefs about himself and his vision of himself. And, dare I say it, that's a requirement for all of us.

Dictionary.com describes tenacity as: "The quality of being tenacious or of holding on fast as in persistence."

I would add to that description "*until the task finished.*"

When you think of somebody who has tenacity, you think of somebody who is determined to finish the job.

What do you think of when you hear 'tenacity?' Do you think of somebody who keeps going no matter what? Do you think of someone who is disciplined and steadfast in their commitment?

To me, 'tenacity' is not just grabbing hold of something and staying with it. It means having the tendency to do *whatever* it takes to see that thing through.

The tendency to step up and willingly go after your dreams, goals, and desires only comes from the inner pull and something called discipline.

Discipline is a nasty word to a lot of people because when we think about it, we think about how much of it we don't have. We often think about how we fell off of our diets and our exercises and our reading and/or whatever it was that we committed to in the past. We think about the times where we didn't get the results we intended, even though we thought we "committed" to it. And that doesn't make us feel good about ourselves.

Instead it starts the downward, internal spiral that I spoke about earlier.

But, as with everything in this book, there is a simple way to change our actions with regard to *discipline*. How do we do that?

What Is Discipline, Really?

There are many definitions of what 'discipline' is. In my view, discipline is simply doing the prescribed activity exactly as prescribed, no matter what, even and especially when it's difficult.

If you take a look at that statement, it says it all, doesn't it? It doesn't say *wanting* to do the activity or *starting* to do it. It says *doing* the prescribed activity.

Let's break this definition down so that we can get some clarity on it, and you can apply it to the things that you want to do.

When I was a little boy, my dad used to build model airplanes and cars with me. I remember one time he brought home a model car and set it down on the table in front of me.

He said: "Okay. What's the first thing we should do?"

I, being only seven or eight years old, grabbed the box and started to tear into it.

He laughed out loud and said: "Slow down, son." Then he took the box and placed it on the table in front of me again. "First," he said, "let's look at the box. The box is going to tell you a lot about what's inside."

And sure enough, as I looked at the box, there was a picture of the model car it contained. On the side, it showed some of the special features and it showed some of the steps to put it together.

My father said: "You've got to learn to do this with everything you come in contact with. Look at it first. Observe it and see what you can learn by looking at it." My father waited a moment while I examined the box further.

"Okay," he said then. "Now let's open it."

I grabbed the box again and was about to start tearing into it when he immediately stopped me with a kind, gentle smile on his face. My father always had an encouraging way about him.

Now he said: "Watch this." He got a knife from the kitchen drawer, cut the plastic wrapping along the seams very carefully, and took the plastic off. Then the box slipped open smooth and easy. "You want to make sure that you don't destroy the box," he explained, "because you're going to need it to put the pieces back in when you're not working on the car."

After that, he said, "Okay. What's next?"

I, of course, started to take all the pieces out of the box and lay them out in front of me. But he stopped me again! "Always, always, always find and read the instructions," my father said. "Most people read the instructions last. The instructions will tell you exactly what to do. If you follow them exactly then you're going to get the desired result."

This went on until we finally sat down and started to put the pieces together.

Those lessons that he taught me have stayed with me my whole life. My dad had a system— a syntax of how to do things. Whether it was building a car, writing a paper for school, preparing for an exam, or anything at all, I've always followed my dad's prescription for getting started and staying with it. And it's always paid off.

If you don't have a prescription for what to do, whether it's from yourself or someone else, you've already shot your chances of following through in the foot.

Imagine if I had *not* followed this series of steps. If I had ripped into the box and started grabbing pieces and trying to figure out how they went together without reading the instructions or knowing what the end product was supposed to look like, what do you suppose would have happened?

Here's what I think: there's a good chance I would never have finished the model. Because I didn't have all the information I needed in the beginning, I would have decided it was "too hard" and eventually given up. Because I didn't even plan ahead for where to put the model and its pieces when I took a break, I wouldn't even have had a box to put them back into!

When something is prescribed it already has a plan in place, so you don't have to make things up.

Having a prescription is the very first step to discipline.

You'll find that for nearly anything you undertake in life, there are countless sources of information available about how to do it. These sources will tell you exactly what the completed task looks like, and exactly what steps you must take to take that outcome. The fine print may include important things you need to know about the requirements, pitfalls, risks, tips, and tricks of undertaking this goal.

By reading all of those and putting together your own personalized "instruction manual," you can ensure that you know the very best way to obtain a goal, from start to finish. You can also make sure it is a goal you *really want to* undertake—not one which contains surprises that you might not want in your life after all. By performing this step first, you can ensure that you finish whatever you start.

Putting together your very own step-by-step instructions is the first step. The second step is *doing the prescribed activity.*

Having a plan or prescription is one thing, but that's just knowledge. It's just information. And knowledge or information that is not acted upon is just words and pictures.

Granted, those words and pictures carry along with them an emotion or feeling. But still, nothing is going to get done if you don't do anything about your plan.

This is where your integrity comes in, and your references for *doing* versus just contemplating.

Remember, there are two types of doing. There's action, and there is activity. Action is doing something once, twice, or a few times. Activity, on the other hand, is rehearsing the action over and over again until you surpass your goals and your desired outcome.

If you go to the gym and I tell you that in order to build your biceps, you must lift 30 pounds 15×10 times in a row, then that is the prescription that I'm giving you. And if you do it, you're going to get a result. But this result is not going to be a result that exceeds your wildest goals forever.

The result is going to be temporary. If you stop performing the activity, your biceps will begin to shrink. Or, if you're trying for another type of goal, your skills will become outdated, etc.. When you are no longer performing the activity, you are no longer meeting or exceeding your goal.

Often the activity needed to achieve your result is going to have some pain along with it. In the case of lifting the weight, if you do it once or twice, you're gonna have sore muscles the next day. Because the human brain likes to avoid pain, this means that the likelihood of you going back into the gym and performing the activity again is greatly reduced.

But that muscle is only going to grow if you go to the gym three or four times a week and repeat the exercise until the muscle has grown to the point that you're satisfied.

Activity means rehearsing the action over and over and over and over again...

No Matter What

Once you understand this, and once you've committed to completing this activity, the next piece is doing it *no matter what.*

Especially when it's difficult.

This is how real results happen. This is where the brain gets trained. This is where the muscles get trained to continue no matter what. This means that, no matter what pops up in the form of obstacles, fear, setbacks, or roadblocks, you will find a way to get it done— no matter what.

When something shows up that hinders you going forward— whether it's physical pain or emotional pain, perceived obstacles or real obstacles— when you stop and do it anyway, you send a clear-cut message to yourself, to other people, and to the world around you: you are going to see this through and you're going to get the results that you intend to get.

The amazing thing about this is that it builds your beliefs about yourself, your integrity, and ultimately your character. Each and every time you get something done *no matter what*, you now have that experience of yourself. You have experienced and proven to yourself that you are someone with high integrity, high ability, and high discipline.

Each time you get it done *no matter what*, it becomes easier to do so in the future. You are teaching yourself, as well as the world around you, that that's the kind of person you are.

This is where progress is made, character is built, and results are produced.

It's not incremental. It's geometric. Because the next time you step to the plate, the next time you step up to do that very task you have a reference for having done it even when it's hard. Your nervous system will then find the upcoming actions easier and more automatic.

This is how anybody, whether they know it or not, builds tenacity. Doing something despite the hardships in front of you is the key to change and results.

You may be thinking to yourself at this point: "Well, Joseph, if I could get myself to do the hard things when I don't want to do them or when I don't feel like doing it or when something gets in my way, then I wouldn't need you or this silly book."

Not to worry. I'm going to give you a process that you can use to help you improve your discipline. But...you're going to have to have the discipline to do it!

You're going to have to work at it, and you're going to have to apply it even and *especially* when it's difficult.

The good news is it's not going to be that difficult. This process is fairly quick with regard to creating the change inside yourself, creating the tendency to step up and do what is necessary.

But...you have to actually perform this process!

Here it is.

Success Exercise, Part 1

Building up a track record of success to prove to yourself that you have discipline may sound intimidating to you. It may sound like a lot of work! But in reality, you have already *done* a tremendous amount of work. You just haven't taken the time to acknowledge or appreciate it yet. That's what we're going to do right now.

I'd like you to spend the next ten minutes writing down *every success of yours that you can think of.* Remember, these go all the way back to when you learned to walk and talk and read and write. They can be as big or as small as you want. Successfully brushing your teeth and eating breakfast this morning definitely counts.

The important thing is, *you must handwrite these successes.* That is, you must use a pen or pencil to write them in a journal, or in this book. That's because the movement of your hand and body is important to incorporating these into your nervous system.

What is the purpose of this exercise? We are going to rapidly remind your nervous system of exactly how successful and disciplined you are. Once we have strengthened the neural pathways through thinking about this question and writing out the answers, your brain will be quicker to associate the concept of "you" with "success" and "discipline."

Learning to do and succeed at new things will now seem much easier now that your brain has been reminded of everything you have already accomplished.

So let's take an intermission to spend ten minutes writing down every success of your own that you can think of.

When you're done, pat yourself on the back and praise yourself enthusiastically. Remember, completing this exercise is one more success!

My Successes (Day 1, Part 1)

_____

_____

_____

_____

_____

_____

_____

_____

_____

_____

Discipline is a Skill

Now that you have graciously reminded yourself of how successful you really are, how do you feel? Do your dreams and goals feel less daunting now that you remember all that you have accomplished? Does it feel easier to get up off the couch and do the next thing—whatever that may be—to get you closer to your goals?

Congratulations. You have taken a big step toward acquiring discipline, simply by completing that writing exercise.

Having discipline sets in motion the tendency to stick with something and finish it all the way through. It's something that I call "the discipline loop."

Look at the diagram below and notice how one thing feeds into the other to create a perpetual motion human being who produces results:

Discipline Loop

Activity (repetition of action) is the precursor to any skill set. (Unconscious competence) Skill sets create Beliefs (unquestioned certainty) Beliefs are the precursor to activity, etc.

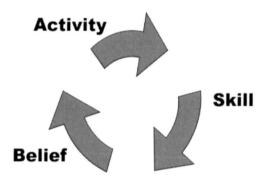

Activity

Skill

Belief

Notice how *activity* is at the top of the loop. Remember, anything that is repeated will become a habit. Any habit that is reinforced will become automatic.

This is how you've learned how to ride a bicycle, drive a car, tie your shoes, etc.. For anything that you can do well, you've done it over and over again, repeatedly, and so it became an automatic part of who you are.

Before you tie your shoes, you don't have to think about it. Before you drive a car, ride a bicycle, or any of those things that you are really good at, you don't have to think about it.

So as long as that works, let's utilize it to create momentum. Once you've done something over and over again, you will create a *skill*.

A skill is any activity that becomes automatic. Any activity that becomes unconsciously competent within your nervous system. The truth of the matter is you have thousands of skills, but you don't ever think about them.

But know this: when you build a skill called discipline, it will help you accomplish anything and everything you desire.

As you develop a skill, you also develop a belief about that activity, and a belief in yourself and your surroundings. I believe that you can accomplish this new skill called discipline, because you have developed skills before. All of this happens unconsciously without you noticing it. But knowing that this process happens will motivate you to continue the process.

This process will create brand new neural pathways and associations in your nervous system and in your mind. Your brain will create new connections and think differently.

Remember: the thinking process creates emotion by sending out electrical impulses, as well as different substances and chemicals that cause you to feel a certain way and behave a certain way.

Understanding this loop will help you understand where you're going and give you encouragement when it comes time to undertake the necessary activity to produce whatever result that you want to have.

Obviously, I'm intellectualizing this now to encourage you. But the reality is that you don't have to know all of this and how it works for it to work.

Just like the bee gathering nectar, you simply perform the activity and results will follow.

This loop I have described of action→ belief→ more action is sometimes called the "personal development loop" because, as you are growing your skills, you're also growing as a person.

This is always necessary because *as you develop into the person that you want to become, you also have to learn and apply new skills.*

Maybe you think you already have all the skills you need to reach your goals. If that's true, why haven't you reached them yet?

The hard and yet glorious truth is that there are more skills in our lives—in *everyone's* lives—than we ever realize. There are "soft" social skills that teach us how to build relationships with people and get the results we want from our relationships. There are discipline skills that tell us how to manage ourselves and get the results we want from our own actions on a consistent basis. There are business, legal, and finance skills that tell us how to handle money and make more of it.

Some people who set out to reach a goal without reading the instructions find this surprising, discouraging, and ultimately do not reach their goals because of that. But the truth is, this is a wonderful thing! It means that *literally everything is a learned skill.* There is no personality trait, talent, or advantage which is beyond your ability *to learn.*

And that is why building discipline as your very first, foundational skill is so important. Once discipline is established in your nervous system, it will allow you to gain any and every other skill you choose.

Perhaps the greatest benefit of all with regard to this discipline loop is that you develop stronger beliefs in other areas of your life as well.

Remember that your ability to have integrity is based on your beliefs about yourself, about other people and about the world around you. Once you start to develop more skills and believe in yourself more, you will also recognize the discipline and the tenacity in others around you. The world will become a more opportune place for you because you start to believe that anything is possible.

In fact, anything *is* possible because you have the magic bullet that will allow you to create anything that you want. History is replete with examples of men and women who stepped up to the plate and saw it through until they got results.

Virtually every invention, every piece of technology, every system, and every accomplishment that affects our world today was preceded by a period of tenacity and discipline. It's those unreasonable people who refused to listen to the reasoning of why they should give up, and who chose to listen to themselves and follow their dreams instead, who have made the biggest impact on our lives today.

It's also important to point out that once you believe, it gives you more certainty to take more action, which in turn gives you more certainty to learn another skill which, in turn creates another belief and so on and so on.

The loop will continue to go and grow.

Empirical Evidence

I want you to realize that all success is built on success. No matter what it is and what the accomplishment might be, it stands on the shoulders of the successes that came before.

We call this "empirical evidence." Empirical evidence is "information that verifies truth." It is hard proof, received by the senses, which shows us that something is definitely true. In the case of discipline, our past successes are our empirical evidence. These successes prove that we are disciplined and able to acquire any new skill we might desire.

When the space shuttle leaves the launch pad and heads for outer space, it succeeds because it is built on the successes of years and years of disciplined individuals who stuck with it. From the successes of today's engineers during their school days to the successes of generations of rocket scientists past, each success proved that another, greater success was possible. And because of that proof, the successes kept building on each other.

The Wright brothers stuck with their ideas and, because of their first success at Kitty Hawk, others were able to build and improve on their inventions. As a result, other airplanes were created and as a result, new means of cutting through our air and traveling across continents were created.

Past successes are empirical evidence that future success is possible. As a result of all the efforts and the successes of those before us, we now have a space station and international airlines.

The same holds true for virtually everything in your life, and mine.

So let's focus on building some empirical evidence that success is possible for you.

You have a lifetime full of accomplishments and successes that you have no doubt forgotten about. For the most part, all of us take for granted all the things that we can do because of the successes that we've had in life.

Something as simple as your success in being able to stand up and walk is what allows you to run. Your success in being able to ride a bicycle is what allows you to drive a car. You have a rich, rich, rich history of successes.

It's critical that you are aware of your successes. Searching for and finding them works to ignite your nervous system, build self-certainty, and instill confidence. The searching process and the writing process will rewire your brain and nervous system for greater discipline and self-belief.

We are now going to repeat the exercise from earlier. We will get you into the habit of building strong discipline and self-consistency by repeating this exercise each day for the next five days.

Success Exercise, Part 2

In this next exercise, take a few moments to write a list of everything that you have been successful at. You can go back as far as you like, and it doesn't have to be in chronological order.

At first, you will probably list the big things. You may soon feel like you run out.

This doesn't mean that you don't have a lot of past successes. It just means that you probably haven't thought of them for a while and because you haven't thought of them, they're buried in your unconscious mind.

You haven't paid attention to these past successes. They have become less impactful on your nervous system. Perhaps you've graduated from high school or college, bought a new car or fixed an old one, learned how to play an instrument, learned how to cook a dish, or won a sporting event or contest. All of these are great!

The brain doesn't care whether the success is big or little. Any success will register as a success. And the more you look for it and find them, the more certainty you build inside yourself.

Instead of only listing the miraculous things and the things that stand out, I want you to list any and every success you can think of. No matter how simple or "small" it is. It doesn't matter if you feel like it's not worthy of listing. List it anyway.

You learned how to ride a bicycle. You took the trash out this morning. You graduated from third grade. The point is to search and find any and everything that you became successful at.

Leave the rest to your unconscious mind. It will make sense of all these successes, and to add each one to your integrity bank account.

Here are the 7 rules for this exercise:

1. Write this out in your journal or in this book. No computers, cell phones, or tablets allowed. You must hand write this list. This movement of your body is necessary to maximize the change in your brain!

2. Write for ten minutes straight. Do not stop.

3. Just list it. You don't have to describe it in detail. Simply listing each item in a few words allows (and requires!) you to find more successes to fill out the list.

4. Your pen or pencil cannot stop moving.

5. No repeating! I don't care how big a given success was; you still have more successes that need to be added to the list.

6. Reward yourself with a pat on the back and a smile when you finish.

7. Repeat this exercise for the next four days with the same guidelines. You are *not allowed to repeat* successes from previous days!

As with all our exercises, it's important that you complete this without concern about whether it's working, or what it's actually doing.

As the book goes on, we will put all the exercises together. But rest assured: while you're doing the exercises, you're actually building connections inside your brain that are going to help you as we stack all of these things up.

So just enjoy this process as you're doing it and allow yourself to dig deep within your own personal history.

You'll be surprised at what you find, and how much you have actually forgotten.

It's also critical that you praise yourself when you've completed this exercise! Praise yourself for having searched so well, and for having done all the things that you just listed.

Remember that your nervous system craves your acknowledgment and recognition. Every single thing within the nervous system responds favorably to praise. Giving yourself acknowledgment and praise is teaching your nervous system to do more of the same discipline and recognition in the future.

And here's the really great part: once you stop working on this task, your brain will keep going. Unconsciously, the brain will continue to search for things. Are you already noticing many previously overlooked successes coming to mind? That's because we got these wheels turning just a few pages back, and they kept going while you were reading this book.

Your belief in yourself and self-certainty will continue to grow. And you can repeat this exercise as often as you like to give yourself that extra boost.

Last but not least, try to have fun.

My Successes (Day 1, Part 2)

_____

_____

_____

_____

_____

_____

_____

_____

_____

_____

_____

_____

_____

_____

My Successes (Day 2)

My Successes (Day 3)

_____

_____

_____

_____

_____

_____

_____

_____

_____

_____

_____

_____

_____

_____

_____

_____

My Successes (Day 4)

_____

_____

_____

_____

_____

_____

_____

_____

_____

_____

_____

_____

_____

_____

_____

My Successes (Day 5)

CHAPTER 5

The Third Element:
Energy

*"If you want to find the secrets of the universe,
think in terms of energy, frequency, and vibration."*
— Nikola Tesla

*"Where attention goes, energy flows; Where
intention goes, energy flows."*
— James Redfield

The next critical element of Magnificence is energy. Without energy, nothing gets done.

Everything on this planet creates and consumes some sort of energy. Every living thing on this planet uses energy to move through time.

The more energy you have, the more successful you will become. The more energy that you have, the more Magnificence you have.

As far back as I can remember, my father was energetic and outgoing. He always seemed to be moving and doing something. Even when he was sitting and relaxing, he seemed to be doing something.

This was not nervous energy. It was more of an intensity of intention. Whatever my father did, he did it with intention, whether it was working, playing, socializing, or sleeping.

My father didn't finish high school as a child. He completed his education while he was raising his family. He went to night school and got his high school education, and then went to night school to get his master's degree. He worked two jobs while he went to night school.

He always seemed to have the energy to play and do things like a really involved dad. Back then, I took it for granted. But as I look back on it now and realize what he did, it blows my mind. I'm proud to say that because he taught his children well that all of us also have a lot of energy.

Even though my father had no medical background to support his beliefs, he strongly believed that your energy came from having a healthy and strong body. Throughout my entire childhood, I never remember my father being sick. I never remembered him having a cold or the flu or anything like that.

Because he was a tenacious man with a lot of integrity, he followed through on his beliefs. He was always moving his body and exercising in some way. And this all became part of the McClendon household. As a matter of fact, my father created an exercise routine for the whole family.

I remember there were certain things that we had to do every day. 50 push-ups, 50 squats, 50 sit-ups, and 50 jumping jacks. There were no exceptions, and they had to be done every single day.

My father would come home late at night from one of his jobs or school and check to see if we had checked off on the family list that we had done our exercises. If we hadn't, he would wake our asses up to do our exercises.

I remember hating it at the time. I remember feeling like he was unreasonable for doing this. But after a while, we didn't question it. We got it done ourselves so he wouldn't wake us up.

As much as I despised it then, not a day goes by now that I don't appreciate the fact that he taught me to take care of my body and take care of myself. I give him so much credit for the energy I still have to this day.

What is Energy?

Let's take a look at what energy really is, so that you'll understand how to create more of it for yourself. And don't worry—I'm not going to recommend that you get out and do all of those exercises that I did! I'm gonna show you a much simpler way to produce energy, starting with your brain.

First and foremost, it's important to understand that energy is just electricity. Everything functions on electricity. Every single cell in your body has an electrical charge in it, and this actually creates electricity.

Every plant or animal has some level of electricity coursing through it. The lack of energy is a lack of life. There are instruments that measure the amount of electricity that courses through our bodies at all times.

We've all seen an electroencephalography machine, otherwise known as an EEG machine, wired up to somebody's head in a science documentary or sci-fi movie. We've all seen electrocardiograms, or EKG/ECG machines, beeping out the heartbeat of the person that is hooked up to.

What most of us don't notice is that the line on the ECG screen measures the amount of electricity being produced by the person's heart. When that charge goes away, both of those lines flatline and there's no more life.

Now, obviously we don't just want to pump electricity into our bodies. In fact, hitting our bodies with electricity from the outside will damage their ability to produce electricity on the inside. Sometimes fatally. This is how electrocution usually kills: it disrupts the heart's own electrical activity.

We don't want to apply electricity to our bodies from the outside. We want to help our body make more electricity from the inside.

This is a simplification of the biology involved, but a useful simplification: the more electricity your body can produce, the more energy you have. The more energy you have, the more you feel able to get things done, and the more integrity you have. And when you have more integrity, you also have more energy, because your brain mobilizes your body more easily. It's a never-ending cycle.

So where does energy come from? How is it made? How is it sustained? And how is it distributed?

We all produce energy within ourselves. When you were first conceived, your mom and your dad each gave you a little piece of their electricity, contained in their sperm and egg cells, which combined to make your life. And as your cells divided and you grew, each new cell was capable of creating electricity. As your body grew, so did your energy.

What's important to know is that those cells dividing caused movement.　And that movement is what creates more electricity. When we move our bodies in any way, our body generates more and more energy that we can use to accomplish our goals.

There are two ways to explain this. There's a simple metaphor which relies on a machine that we already know something about and which is quite easy to understand. There's also a slightly more complex explanation that is closer to how these processes really work in our bodies.

I am going to give you both explanations here today. To begin with, we will discuss the complexities of how your body really works, and why movement energizes you.

Then we will discuss a simple metaphor which anyone can remember to encourage you to keep "turning your engine over."

Movement: The Metabolism and Neurology

Obviously, the human body doesn't work exactly like a car. It would be nice if it did though, right? Just switch out any old or broken parts...

But in reality, our bodies are complex biological machines that allow us to do amazing things like feeling, thinking, and experiencing sensation and emotion.

Our bodies make energy in little tiny organelles inside our cells called "mitochondria." They are the machines that turn air, water, and food into energy for us.

Mitochondria are the first piece to the puzzle of how movement creates energy for us. Because it turns out, mitochondria can get lazy. If we never move or exercise to place demands on our mitochondria, they become straight-up couch potatoes. Like undisciplined kids, they sit on the couch playing video games all day instead of working hard to turn air, water, and food into all the energy we could ever want.

How do you get your mitochondria into shape? You discipline them. You set high expectations. You push them to produce more and more energy faster and faster on a daily basis.

This, it turns out, is what my father's strict daily exercise routine was doing for us. By constantly demanding so much of our bodies, we were building muscles full of lots and lots of mitochondria, which were tested and kept up to scratch.

It turns out that when we demand more from our mitochondria, such as by exercising, they actually do get stronger and more efficient at producing energy. So instead of "saving our energy" for vital tasks, we ought to be asking "how can we make *more* energy than we're making right now?" And the answer to that is, by moving around and exercising!

Moving our bodies also creates energy in two other important ways.

For one thing, it turns out that our muscles act as natural pumps for our blood vessels. Our blood vessels and lymphatic systems are the systems our bodies use to deliver cleansing and nourishing water to our cells, and to carry away toxins and waste products that gunk up the works.

It turns out that when we move, our muscles act as pumps to speed up the action of this system. The more we move around each day, the faster our cells receive life giving water and get the gunk cleaned out of their cellular machinery.

This alone is a good reason to take a walk, do some cleaning, or even do a silly little dance every so often throughout the day. You don't need to push your muscles to their limits to gain this key benefit of movement. It'll probably even perk your mitochondria up a bit as well.

The third major benefit of movement comes from our nervous systems. That is to say, our brains.

You may have heard that the nervous system generates electricity to tell our muscles what to do. Well, that's true. But it turns out that the process also works in reverse! When we engage in activities that engage our muscles, such as dancing, this stimulates all kinds of areas in our brains. It stimulates the nerves and muscles and mitochondria all throughout our bodies, too.

In short, moving around and dancing energizes us!

Scientific studies have shown huge benefits to adding even a little bit of movement to your day. People who exercise more have more energy, people who walk more live longer, and people who dance can have greater mental acuity and even stave off age-related degeneration of their brains.

So if you're in a rut or feel just plain sapped, try moving around a little. You don't have to run a marathon or perform some dignified, serious workout to gain the benefits of doing a little happy dance in your office.

Movement: Charging Your Alternator

My dad taught me about cars, and that's often how I think about anything that I need to understand or explain in life. In the case of movement and energy the analogy is obvious: just like us, cars run out of batteries if they sit around without moving for a while.

Your car engine may run on gasoline, just as our bodies run on food. But your engine can't start if your alternator battery is drained. Why is that? Why isn't the fuel alone enough to get your car moving?

Well, the answer is that your car needs a spark of electricity to get it moving. That's the spark that lights up the gasoline and gets your engine pumping. If the car has a dead battery, it can't get moving.

The genius of our cars—and our bodies—is that the electricity we need to get moving is *created* by movement.

For a car, the battery is charged when the engine runs. The movement of the cylinders and the wheels turns a generator which charges up your battery any time the car is moving.

However, if the car sits for a long time without moving—especially if it's expending electricity, like when you leave the headlights or the radio on in a parked car—the battery will get drained. Without movement, it can't be charged up. When you try to get the car moving again, you may just find that you can't. It doesn't have the electricity it needs to start up.

Think of your body in the same way. If you are sitting around thinking a lot, it's kind of like sitting in a parking lot with your lights on. If you don't throw some movement in there, you will drain your battery and find it harder to get started doing anything at all. But if you move around throughout the day, you'll find that you have *more* energy to do anything you want to do.

Don't think of movement as "expending your energy." Think of it as "charging your battery." That is closer to the scientific truth.

Backed By Science

I recently met and worked with an amazing man named Dr. Jerry Tennant. We became friends and worked together at one of our large seminars. I went through his certification course a couple months back, and the information he shared with me was in line with my father's beliefs and my own beliefs. More than that, he had done something amazing with this information.

Dr. Tennant was one of the original creators of Lasik surgery. He also pioneered outpatient procedures so that people didn't have to spend time in the hospital after their surgery.

Unfortunately, at the height of his career, Dr. Tennant developed a very serious illness. He had a virus in his brain, and nobody could figure out what it was. It started to rob him of his energy and of his faculties. It started to rob him of his memory and of his ability to function at the level of a physician. He became bedridden for six years.

During that time, he started asking different questions and trying to feed his brain in an effort to retain what he had left. In his studies, he started to recognize that all cells need electricity to heal themselves. Cells use chemical energy, but one important form of that is *electrochemical* energy.

This is the type of energy that cells produce and use to send important signals, perform important functions, and just generally stay alive. In fact, up to 25% of the air you breathe and the food you eat is used as fuel to create electrochemical energy to keep your cells alive and healthy!

Dr. Tennant soon realized that if cells didn't have the proper amount of electricity then they couldn't repair and replace themselves.

With this knowledge, he set out to find the exact amount of electricity that cells need, and he mapped out the path of electricity from one's muscles to specific areas of the body. Using his findings, he then created a system and a machine that distributed the exact right amount of electricity to the exact right spots in the body so that the cells would have electricity to heal themselves.

He also started to realize that there are certain things that block our cells from producing electricity. He realized that without movement causing our neurons and muscles to fire electrical impulses, the production of electricity would slow down greatly or stop. He applied this knowledge to himself and within a very short amount of time, his body started to respond.

His immune system was restored, his pains and ailments were eliminated, and he regained all his faculties. Now he runs a successful clinic in Dallas where he helps patients with their health challenges.

There is much much more to Dr. Tennant's philosophies and the work that he's done. For more information, check him out on YouTube or go online and look up the Tennant Institute. It will blow you away.

The important thing to know is that even without his machines or that technology, your body knows what to do to protect, heal, and elevate itself. After all, if you cut yourself, you don't have to tell the wound to heal. All you have to do is give it the proper time and nutrition, keep it clean, and it will heal itself.

The same goes for creating energy. You don't have to know what it's doing. You just have to give the body what it needs, and it will produce all the energy that you need. So it's important to understand what the body needs in order to produce more energy.

It's not necessary to full-on change every aspect of your life to produce results. Remember, small shifts now will build on each other and create geometric growth and huge change along the way. A one-degree shift every single day adds up to 365° in one year! That's full-circle and then some.

What I'm going to suggest to you is simple. For several years I have taught and hosted health retreats in Geneva, Switzerland and La Marbella, Spain. I would bring people in for five days straight, and I would take them through a powerful process. Each day we would eat a specific way. We would move our bodies in a specific way. We would focus our brains in a certain way. And at the end of five days, the changes were nothing short of a miracle.

The best part about it was after everyone left, most of them continued to practice at least some of what they learned and what they experienced. To this day, one of my greatest joys is hearing from people about how their lives have drastically changed.

The Six Elements of Abundant Energy

There are six things that have a big influence on how much energy our body can produce. All of these are either used as fuel by our bodies to create energy, or as signals to tell our body how much energy they should create. These six elements are:

1. The air we breathe

2. The water we drink

3. The food we eat

4. The thoughts we think

5. The moves we make

6. The words we speak

As basic as these elements are, paying attention to any one of them—or better yet, to *all* of them—will significantly enhance your energy.

Remember you don't have to make Herculean change to experience this. Just do a little bit at a time and you'll start to notice a difference. You'll sleep differently. You'll have more energy, discipline, and tenacity.

Here is a brief breakdown of each one of the components and what to do about it.

Follow these simple suggestions and you will get results. What's even better is that you will develop habits that will take you further and faster towards the new you.

The Air We Breathe

You might be thinking to yourself that this is a no-brainer. Of course we need air to stay alive! Why would this even be mentioned? Breathing is the most fundamental thing that we do.

But upon closer examination, you'll recognize that most people are only breathing at half of their full capacity. High-performance athletes receive special training in how to move more air through their bodies so that they can generate more energy. Clinical studies are also now beginning to show that people who practice "diaphragmatic breathing"—a type of deep-breathing exercise—heal faster and more effectively from all kinds of illnesses and injuries.

Why is it that most of us don't breathe at our full capacity? It turns out that stress impacts our ability to breathe. When we get stressed, our muscles—including the muscles around our lungs—tighten up. Our lungs don't expand as much when we breathe in, and they don't contract as much to expel carbon dioxide when we breathe out either. No wonder many of us are in states of impaired breathing!

Our cells need oxygen to create energy. It's that simple. If they don't have the oxygen, they can't produce electricity. If they can't produce electricity, they can't send electricity throughout the rest of your body. Worse yet, when your breathing is impaired, your cells will function at just half of their capacity and may even perish.

Because breathing is the most important thing that you do, it makes sense to focus on breathing more efficiently as your first step to having more energy. Breathing is key to your ability to become more Magnificent.

I'm purposely putting a page break here so that you cannot read ahead before you finish what I'm going to ask you to do. It's important that you just follow these instructions to learn something about yourself.

Breathing Exercise (Part 1 of 3)

Go stand in front of a mirror. As you stand there, I want you to take five deep breaths. Breathe in as much air as your lungs can hold and then let the air out.

As you do this, I want you to observe how your body moves as you take those deep breaths.

Close the book now and go and do that exercise.

Breathing Exercise (Part 1 of 2)

Welcome back.

What did you notice about your body as you took those deep breaths? What parts of your body moved as you took those breaths? For most people, you'll notice that your chest comes up and out, your shoulders come back, your head comes back, and your stomach goes in.

This is a typical way of breathing for most people. If this is what happened to your body, *congratulations*, you are like most people on the planet.

The bad news is, you're only getting about half of the oxygen capacity that your lungs were designed to provide you.

If you look at the way the lungs are shaped in the body, they're like triangles. They're bigger on the bottom and smaller on the top. You were designed in a very specific way to get the optimal amount of oxygen into your system every time you breathe.

Your lungs do not have muscles. They are operated by a big muscle at the bottom of your lungs, called your diaphragm. That diaphragm does two things, every minute, for your entire life: it pulls down and pushes up.

This movement does several things. As your diaphragm pulls down, it creates a vacuum in your lungs which pulls air in. As it pushes up, it creates pressure in your lungs which pushes carbon dioxide—used air that has had all the energy taken out of it—out. That is the inhale-and-exhale process that all mammals and reptiles do.

Inside your lungs, you have little bags called alveoli. When the air comes in, these sacks grab the oxygen molecules and take them into your bloodstream. From there, they go to your cells, which will turn them into energy.

When the diaphragm pulls down, it creates a vacuum in your chest which pulls air into the bottom parts of your lungs. It also pushes your abdominal organs out and down to make room for that sweet, sweet air.

This means that as you inhale your stomach should poke out, not pull in. For most people when they inhale their stomach pulls in. Many people think this is normal because they think it is the chest that is supposed to expand. In fact, this means that your muscles are tight and your abdominal organs aren't moving the way they should to allow your lungs to expand all the way.

If you noticed that your stomach was pulling in instead of poking out when you breathed in, it means that as you're inhaling, your diaphragm is moving up instead of down.

As it moves up, it's creating pressure and collapsing the bottom third of your lungs.

Your lungs are bigger at the bottom. The bottom third occupies about 50% of the oxygen capacity of your lungs. This is where the biggest concentration of the alveoli is.

Needless to say, if we want to get your lungs operating at full capacity, we have to change a couple of things about the way you breathe.

Breathing Exercise (Part 3 of 3)

We can easily improve your breathing simply by allowing your stomach to come out as you take a deep breath. This "belly breathing" has been taught as part of meditation to strengthen the mind and concentration for thousands of years.

Now, go to the mirror. Practice taking a deep breath in and allowing your stomach to come out.

Watch as this happens, and you'll start to notice that you're getting more and more oxygen with each inhale. You'll also probably start to notice that you might feel a little euphoric and maybe even a little lightheaded.

That will go away in time, but it's a clear sign that your brain and your body are getting more oxygen!

When does your brain have the most imagination and fertility? When is it that your body is healing and repairing itself? When you are asleep!

This is the time that your body uses to repair itself and create the compounds and solutions that it needs to carry on living for the next day. During this time, your brain is at its most fertile and your imagination is most expansive.

We've all had fantastic dreams where we could fly and do all kinds of things that we would normally never think about. One reason for this, and one reason for our ability to heal ourselves during that time, is because when we lay down, we automatically breathe using our diaphragm the right way. This means we are automatically giving ourselves more oxygen.

Don't believe me? Watch a baby or a puppy while they sleep. The only thing that moves on them is their little tummies moving up and down. Their shoulders aren't moving, and their heads aren't moving.

Babies and puppies have not learned to stress breathe yet. They're breathing correctly. We need to be copying them.

The air we breathe is the first thing on this list for a reason. Practice breathing like this over and over again, and you'll start to see massive results in your energy.

It's free, it's easy, and the benefits are astounding.

The Water We Drink

Just like breathing, this one seems basic. But you would be amazed at how many people fall way short of getting the benefits of this essential component of life.

Water makes up 75% of who you are. Water makes up 75% of this glorious earth that we inhabit. It is the one true common denominator that all living things need to thrive. Some don't even need air, but they do need water!

It's important to understand that water is a critical component of our energy. Water conducts electricity and is the body's natural solvent for electricity-carrying molecules. With the exception of the oils that our bodies produce, pretty much everything else is water-soluble. Water regulates our temperatures, it carries impurities out of our bodies, and carries minerals and nutrients to our vital organs.

Most people are dehydrated. Even though they may drink lots of different liquids, the amount of plain water that most people drink is staggeringly low. Ironically, much of the water we do drink is used to produce the energy needed to filter water out of the liquids that we do drink like coffee, soft drinks, alcohol, processed juices, etc.. Non-water beverages make up as much as 75% of the total liquid intake of the vast majority of the population of developed countries.

Sadly, a great deal of the water that most people consume is contaminated with chemicals and even plastic particles from the containers that they're stored in. Also, the amount and the quality of the water that most people intake is poor.

Shifting this one area just a little bit makes a huge, huge difference in people's lives. I could talk for a full day on this subject. And as a matter of fact, at my retreat, I do. I bring in a water expert who does demonstrations and shows people the value of drinking high-quality water and the grim reality of the water that they are drinking.

It's pretty scary but the great news is there's an easy, simple fix.

For many years, the standard rule was you should be drinking eight glasses of water every day. Most people fall way short of that amount.

For a lot of us, that goal might be unrealistic. Not to mention one would have to stay pretty close to a bathroom if we drank that much water! Unless you have an exceptionally large bladder and holding capabilities, you'd be in and out of the bathroom at least eight times a day. That formula also does not take into consideration the size and age of individuals.

As a rule of thumb, you can get enough water by drinking a glass every two hours. You can use your cell phone to set a timer to remind you. It's a powerful, simple way of getting enough water into you.

The great news is that after a few days of cleaning your body out, you won't be as dependent on coffee or stimulants. Your body will produce natural energy and you won't need to get yourself jacked up on artificial stimulants like caffeine.

It takes about a week for our body to adapt to this routine. After that, your cravings for sweet drinks and caffeinated drinks will start to dissipate. You'll find yourself sleeping better as well as thinking more clearly.

The mechanics are simple. Once you start eliminating the toxins from your body, your body will function much better. The internal circuitry that your electricity passes through will be unencumbered.

As an extra added benefit, if you're seeking to lose weight, drinking water is a huge factor. One of the ways weight leaves our body is through our urine. Some of us may also mistake thirst for hunger when we are dehydrated, eating when our body actually wants to drink water.

If you're moving your body, the fat will come off of your body and into your bloodstream, then into your bladder where it will be eliminated. So the more water you drink, the more pathways the fat has to leave your body.

Dehydration is the enemy of progress with regard to energy, health, fitness, and weight loss.

The type of water you drink also plays a huge role in your energy. All water may be created equally, but it certainly does not reach your lips equally. There are so many toxins and additives in our water these days that it can be downright dangerous at times.

Most people think that drinking bottled water is the answer to eliminating toxins. The challenge is often that bottled water has been processed before it goes into the bottle and chemicals like fluoride and other purifying agents have been used to filter the water. Don't be fooled by the labels and even the claims on the bottle. Unfortunately, advertisers can get away with claiming that their water is natural and from the stream.

It may originally have been from the stream—but by the time it gets to you, it has been altered, and not always for the better.

Water that has been placed in a plastic bottle has generally been sitting in storage or transport for weeks and sometimes even months before you get it. During this time it can go through several different temperature changes, and each time the temperature changes the plastic from the bottle releases some of its integrity into the water. You can taste the plastic in some bottled waters. This is very dangerous because plastics can also be carcinogenic.

The best thing to do is to drink filtered water that has been filtered in front of your eyes. Also, store your water and carry your water in a glass or stainless-steel container. Glass or stainless steel will not leach into the water like plastic will.

The balance of alkaline and acid in the water is important as well. In general, you want to have water that is more alkaline than acidic. Acidic water promotes the growth of bacteria parasites, yeast, and fungus within your bloodstream. Water with a higher alkaline content is much more natural and friendlier to your body and body functions.

In case you didn't know, there are different types of tests and machines that can change the pH balance of the water. This is extremely important because water is made up of three molecules.

I have no doubt that you've heard the formula H2O. Water is made of two molecules of hydrogen—H2—plus one molecule of oxygen, a single O.

The size and diameter of those three molecules together are the exact same size of the pores in our cells. Our cells are, in fact, designed to let in water and very little else.

When water is in its natural form, those H2O molecules are separate and they bounce off each other. This way the cells can absorb the water and distribute it throughout your body.

But the moment you introduce any other substance into that water, those molecules attach themselves to that substance and create clusters. Sometimes this is useful for our bodies, like when our bodies want water to be carrying minerals, nutrients, and chemical messages from our brain. But water will stick to *anything*, helpful or toxic.

This is why coffee, soft drinks, and any solution of water to which color is added remains colored. The water molecules attach themselves to the sugar, dye, or caffeine, and they keep all those substances suspended in that solution. Even substances that are colorless and dissolve into the water are still suspended there because the water molecules attach themselves to the substance. This includes chemicals that are added and the plastics that were leached from the bottle.

These clusters of water + other molecules are now too big to fit through the pores of our cells and bounce off. The cells are now suspended in a kind of toxic soup, waiting for the digestive system to separate the toxins from the water molecules. Obviously, this is not ideal to allow our cells to efficiently take in water and use it to create energy. Clustering of molecules also occurs when water sits for more than a couple of hours without moving.

This is why if it is at all possible you want to drink "ionized" water. Ionization separates the clusters and returns the water to its natural state. It's a simple process, and you can actually taste and feel the difference. The water feels softer and more slippery. This is because your tongue is absorbing the water and it is actually getting wetter.

There are several companies that produce ionizer-filter combinations. I will include some links in the index so you can research the different types of machines and brands.

The really good news is that filtering your own water and ionizing your own water is considerably cheaper than buying bottled water. It's as much as 50% cheaper and it's more convenient because it's right there in your home. And because it's right there in your home and you don't have to go out for it so you're more likely to drink more of it.

So set your phone alarm to go off every two hours, don't drink from untrusted plastic bottled waters, and get an ionizer filter to upgrade your water drinking habits.

Your body will thank you, your health will thank you, and you'll be generating more energy in the process.

The Food We Eat

Here's another subject that I could literally write a whole book on. And as a matter of fact, I did.

Back in 2008, I wrote a book called "Change Your Breakfast to Change Your Life." In that book I talked about what foods to eat, what they do, when's the best time to eat them, and how much to eat.

I'm not going to spend much time on that now, since there is a whole book you can consult on the subject if you want to. Instead, in the interest of keeping it simple, I'm just going to give you some really basic information and offer you a simple solution to get the food that you eat in check.

It is important that you understand what food really is and how your body uses it. Food is nutrition, and nutrition is another word for nutrients. Nutrients are the substances that the cells need and use to create energy and building blocks for new, healthy cells.

Each cell has its own specific job to do within your body. Liver cells have a specific form and function that they need to accomplish their purpose. For that reason, liver cells are very different from the cells that are in your eyes and so on.

Cells perform very specific functions all day and all night long. Some cells also duplicate themselves, producing healthy new cells when growth or healing is needed. This process has been going on since the moment you were conceived.

Cells divide and make new cells. Cells use the nutrients that come into your body to carry out specific tasks. The solutions and compounds that each cell makes are very specific as well. Solutions like saliva, mucus, lymph fluid, blood, urine which carries toxins out of the body, etc..

Now you can understand why it's important to have water to aid in helping these liquids flow through your bloodstream. These fluids also make up the structure of your cells and form different compounds.

We need up to 114 different types of nutrients every single day to function. Each cell needs a fresh new supply of nutrients every single day. If they cannot get those nutrients, they will resort to finding it by any means necessary.

Think of your cells as little tiny individual beings. They are programmed to stay alive by any means necessary. If you have not been supplying your body with the proper amounts and types of nutrients, your cells will go find those nutrients by leaching those nutrients from your storage supplies.

Your storage supplies are your bones, fat, muscles, and organs. Some nutrients can be obtained by breaking down your fat cells, but not all of them. If your body is deprived of a certain nutrient for too long, it will begin to break down your muscles, organs, and bones to stay alive.

If your bones and organs are unable to retain enough nutrients for their own function and are unable to get more nutrients, they will atrophy and die. This process causes many diseases and accelerates aging.

The biggest organ that we all have is our skin. It is one of the first places our cells go to leach nutrients. This is why some people appear to age faster than others. It's because they don't have the proper nutrition to support their cells. Their cells are robbing that nutrition from the skin. The skin cells then can't divide or produce proteins like collagen to stay young and healthy. It's really quite simple when you look at it this way.

Obviously, you want to supply your body with the right amounts and the right types of foods which carry with them the nutrients necessary for your body to function optimally. A good way to look at what to eat is by looking at the composition of your body, and for that matter the composition of the planet.

75% of our planet is covered in water. 75% of your body is made up of water. So it makes sense that 75% of the food that you put in your body should be water-rich foods— like fruits and vegetables. Fruits and vegetables are rich in nutrients such as vitamins and minerals.

I happen to believe that everything that your body needs to thrive either comes growing up out of the ground in a bush, vine, root, plant or bubbling up out of the earth in a stream. And for the life of me, I have never seen a potato chip bush, a French fry vine, or a Coca-Cola stream.

I'm not suggesting that you have to become a vegetarian. I am, however, suggesting that you rethink what you put on your plate and in your mouth. Most people can use their common sense to recognize that eating natural foods is beneficial.

Much of our food now has been mechanized so that, by the time we get our food, it has been processed and many of the nutrients have been stripped out of it. When machines create refined flour or sugar or processed cheeses, for example, one thing they're doing is stripping out many natural substances that are supposed to be there. This doesn't happen when you eat fruits and vegetables.

If you're going to eat meat, just get it from a clean source. The more naturally the animal eats during its life, the more naturally it is raised, and the less it is processed after slaughter, the better.

I happen to believe that we were designed to eat a plant-based diet. 75% of our teeth are designed to grind. These teeth are the same types of teeth that show up in animals that graze and eat plants. The remaining 25% of your teeth are cutting and tearing teeth. Those are for your meat.

So take a look at what is in your diet currently and make the adjustments. It's not that hard, and you'll start to notice the difference in your energy, vitality, and appearance right away.

Lastly, the amount of food that you eat is important as well. The average stomach is about the size of your own fist. If you take your fist and place it on your abdomen, notice how big it is.

Then, when you're making your meals, take a look at the plate and see if the food on your plate is bigger than your fist. If it is, you're overeating. Your stomach will stretch, but when it does, it means you're taxing your entire system. Your body is going to have to work overtime, using more energy, and robbing you of vitality just to digest your food.

Eating smaller portions will give you energy and will keep you from gaining unnecessary weight. The body is a truly remarkable thing, and it knows what to do to heal itself and take care of itself.

If you give it the proper nutrients, it will do the job for you.

The Thoughts We Think

It seems a bit strange to think that we can create energy just by thinking. But it's the absolute truth! The thoughts we think, just the words that we use and the images that we create in our minds, will affect our energy levels tremendously.

Let's talk about the images that you create in your mind. Try to think about something that stresses you out for a moment. You'll probably start to notice your heart race. Maybe you'll feel an uncomfortable feeling in your stomach, and maybe you'll even feel anxious.

This is because your brain is releasing chemicals like adrenaline and testosterone causing you to feel this way. This fear attacks your nervous system as well as your immune system.

Which thoughts are causing you to feel that way? You've probably also noticed that once that feeling goes away, you feel tired and have less energy.

Now let's try the opposite. Think of something that makes you smile, that you're excited about, and makes you happy. You'll probably start to notice a calmness come over your body. You'll probably start to notice that you actually feel more motivated and excited because of these thoughts. This simple exercise should show you that you can create energy and better health through your thoughts.

The challenge is, with so many things bombarding us day in and day out, it's very hard to direct your thoughts for long periods of time. As I'm writing this book, the world is in the middle of the COVID-19 pandemic. People are scared, and people are getting sick all over the world. This might be all people hear about if they watch the news or go on social media.

But there's one thing that all of the professionals, all of the physicians and all of the healthcare professionals agree on: those who are most susceptible to catching the virus are those who have a compromised immune system. That means people with pre-existing conditions, and people who are in poor health. Scientists also agree that stress is a huge contributor to weakening our immune system.

When we have too many stress hormones in our body for a long time, our bodies get the message that they'd better "turn down" our immune systems and healing processes, because we need to conserve our strength. This makes sense if we are in a famine and nutrients are scarce, but not so much in the middle of a contagious disease pandemic.

Stress is just another word for fear. Our challenge is that the media is bombarding us 24 hours a day with the worst possible scenarios and an overwhelming amount of negative news. Because people are so used to getting their information from these sources, they become addicted to bad news. This bad news creates fear and bad thoughts inside of our heads.

Whatever we focus on is what we're going to feel. The stress hormones that are produced from the thoughts we are thinking then have a negative effect on our immune system.

Having said all this, it's important that you practice something called a *directed mind*. This means that you choose what to focus on and what to think.

You choose to put thoughts into your own mind that cause you to have more energy and feel good. No one can do this 24/7, but with practice we can learn to make choices about our thoughts, our activities, and our media consumption that lead us to much happier, more energized lives.

As obvious as this may sound, learn the skill of extreme optimism. This works no matter what is going on in your life. It's not just positive thinking: it's a mind directed towards what is possible and energizing, versus allowing your mind to be hijacked by outside influences and distractions.

Thinking Exercise

Take some time and make a list of all the things that make you happy. Make a list of all the things that are positive and great. Make a list of all the things that you're grateful for. Make a list of all the people that you're grateful for. Make a list of all the blessings that you already have in your life. Remember *as you write, you invite.*

It is critical that you do this because your brain will continue to do it even after you complete the exercise. This will become part of who you are, how you think, and how your body functions. In the end, you'll generate energy and assist your nervous system and your immune system in carrying out its job and making you healthy, happy, and full of energy. You can do this every day if you like.

1. List as many positive things you can think of in your life.

_____

_____

_____

_____

_____

2. List as many things as you can think of that you are grateful for. Include the past and the present.

_____

_____

_____

_____

_____

_____

_____

_____

_____

_____

_____

_____

_____

_____

_____

_____

_____

3. List all the people who you're grateful for. Past and present.

_____

_____

_____

_____

_____

_____

_____

_____

_____

_____

_____

_____

_____

_____

4. List all the blessings that you already have in your life.

_____

_____

_____

_____

_____

_____

_____

_____

_____

_____

_____

_____

_____

_____

_____

_____

The Moves We Make

Once you have those first four elements in place, your body can utilize them to create energy and distribute it throughout your body. Now, movement is how you turn all those elements into electricity.

We addressed earlier in this chapter the important ways in which movement increases our energy. To recap, those are:

1. When we exercise rigorously (or even mildly), we demand more energy from our mitochondria. These little cellular machines that turn air, food, and water into energy our cells can use subsequently become more disciplined, efficient, and capable.

    When we don't make demands on them through movement and exercise, they can become lazy, inefficient, and unproductive.

2. When we move around in any way, the movement of our muscles pumps our veins and lymphatic systems. This makes our bodies more efficient and effective at delivering nurturing, cleansing water and moving out toxic waste that can gunk up our cells and mitochondria.

    Any time we move in any way, we are speeding up the delivery of good stuff to our cells and the removal of bad stuff. Subsequently, our energy levels go up.

3. When we move around in any way, we are stimulating neurons in our brain. This can activate new thoughts and feelings, increase our mental abilities, and even stave off age-related brain degeneration.

It's exactly like that car we talked about. Your car may be powered by gasoline (fuel), but it can't turn the fuel into energy without movement. The engine must have a spark to ignite the fuel to make the pistons go up and down.

But where does the spark come from?

Well, if you know anything about cars, you know that the car has a battery. The battery supplies the electricity that the car needs to get moving. But the battery can't charge itself. It must be charged by the motion of the engine.

When the car is not running—for example when you leave the lights or run the radio on—the battery is being drained without motion to recharge it. If the lights are on and the car is not running, this will eventually drain the battery and your car will be unable to start.

So how *does* the battery get its electricity? How does motion charge that battery up and keep it charged? After all, that car is sitting dormant until you get in and start it up.

When you turn the key, the electricity goes from the battery to the starter. The starter turns the motor over, the motor turns the distributor, the electricity from the battery sends a signal to the coil and the coil produces a spark in the spark plugs. The spark plugs ignite the fuel in the cylinders, the engine turns and powers the wheels. Down the road you go!

The car gets its energy and electricity from something called the alternator. In older cars, it was called a generator. The generator creates electrical energy from movement. It is constantly spinning because it is attached to the engine—powered by the very same force of movement that turns your wheels. Once the engine gets going, it turns the alternator and the alternator creates electricity. This electricity goes to the battery and charges it.

The alternator is always spinning as long as the car is running. If the alternator is spinning, it's generating electricity to charge the battery. Once the battery has received a full charge, it doesn't need to take any more from the alternator, but the alternator nonetheless continues to produce electricity.

Think of your body as working like an automobile. You have to have something that generates electricity, and you have to have a place to store that electricity. The car with its spinning alternator and storage battery is similar to you as a human being, as your movement is what generates electricity.

When you stop moving, your muscles stop generating electricity. Your brain and heart keep going, but brain power and heart power alone can only get us so far. We need *physical* power too. And without movement, even our brain and our heart start to get bogged down.

Our Creator built an amazing system within our bodies. Our muscles are like alternators and generators in our bodies. When we move them, we generate the kind of electricity and chemical energy that we need to *keep* moving.

Fortunately, our Creator set up a process for us to always be moving, even when we're sitting still. The breathing process is the moving process and, at the very least, it's generating enough electricity for you to stay alive.

In this modern day and age, most of our technology is aimed at making life easier for us. Making life easier for us often means we use our bodies less, and as a result, we have a population that has low energy because we're not generating and storing a sufficient amount of energy to keep us going.

This is why substances like coffee and energy drinks have been on the rise for some time now. People are seeking artificial energy by putting things into their bodies, instead of recognizing that all they have to do is move their body and they'll generate more energy.

The entire system works so much better when we use our bodies the way they are intended to be used. When we move around, all our systems run better.

Now don't get it twisted. I'm not telling you that you have to get out and run 10 miles a day, exercise on a treadmill, or lift a bunch of weights to generate the type of energy that I'm talking about. You can accomplish this by simply walking. You can add just a little bit of movement to your day, and it will work wonders.

This effect also has a geometrically stacking effect. The more you move, the more your body will start to crave movement and you'll want to do more of it. The more energy that you generate, the more you'll *want* to generate.

So schedule some time every day where you can walk for at least 15 to 20 minutes. Take the stairs instead of the elevator. Walk the dog a few times to move your body. Take a yoga class. Do some stretching.

Do *anything* as long as you're consistently moving your body. Sitting and thinking—being parked with the lights on, so to speak—for too long drains your energy. It's also important that when you have a meal to move your body a bit once you've completed your meal.

The Words We Speak

Just like the thoughts that we think, the words that we speak have the ability to change our biochemical makeup.

When you hear a joke, those words make you smile and cause your brain to release oxytocin, endorphins, and dopamine. Those chemicals cause you to feel good and form bonds with those around you.

Subsequently, when you hear words that are upsetting, your body will release chemicals that make you feel bad. As a result, your energy level will drop in terms of usable energy towards your goals.

The most powerful words that are spoken are the words that we speak to ourselves. After all, we are our own constant companions. Most people have what I call "the internal dialogue from hell." Sometimes we speak to ourselves in tones that are judgmental and harsh. We may even be our own doomsayers.

The words that we speak to ourselves are not always the same words that we speak out loud. However, the words that we speak out loud can program the words we speak in our minds.

Remember, your brain cannot resist repetition. Anything that is repeated will become a habit. Any habit that is reinforced with praise and appreciation will become automatic. This is the same way we memorize a song or a poem. If we can set up a set of words that will consistently play in the background, these words become like an operating system for our brain.

The most powerful words that you can speak are the words that you use to describe who you are. Even though most of us are not conscious of how we describe ourselves, it is important that you take a look inside and evaluate what you say about yourself.

Go back to the first exercise that we did in Chapter 2 and look at some of the words that you used. They are probably pretty telling as to how you feel about yourself and how you describe yourself.

Your brain doesn't care what you say. It doesn't apply a filter to decide whether your words are right or wrong. Whatever you say to your brain, it will act upon it. So as long as you're saying something anyway, you might as well say the best stuff.

Through a process called "incanting," you can embed any thoughts that you want in your mind. Remember, your psychology is what runs your whole life. And your psychology is simply the underlying, consistent words that you speak to yourself.

Incanting is *not* the same as affirmations. Affirmations are just saying words over and over again, trying to convince yourself of what you're saying. Incanting is the process of saying a specific set of words over and over again, *while* moving your body and creating emotional intensity.

To incant properly, you will want to be bouncing up and down, moving your hands, shaking your ass, dancing, breathing deeply, and speaking loudly. This activity creates energy, releases chemical messengers inside your brain, and opens up both your conscious and your unconscious mind. Incanting allows the meanings of those words to sink deeper into your psychology.

Remember, anything that is repeated will become a habit and a memory. Those memories and experiences will soon become your unconscious beliefs. In turn, they will generate more energy and create a more enthusiastic, optimistic psychology. This in turn will produce more energy for you to use in your daily life.

Silent Exercise

Take a few moments now to be silent. Get yourself somewhere where you don't have radio, TV, or any other words getting broadcast at you in the background. Then put this book down, don't have any outside input at all for three minutes.

As you sit in silence, you'll start to notice that you can hear the voice that is speaking to you inside your head.

Now that you're back to the book, I want you to answer the following questions about that voice:

1. Whose voice is speaking?

2. In general, is the voice optimistic or pessimistic in tone and language?

Now, create a list of words that are powerful, uplifting, and positive to describe yourself. Create as many phrases and you can.

Examples:

- I am healthy, happy, wealthy, and kind. I love myself and I love my life.

- All that I need is within me now and I will prevail some way, somehow.

- At last, the past has passed. I've broken three and one, and now it's time to love myself and really have some fun. A whole new world is on the rise for all of us and I'm the one. Yes, I am the one. I am a beacon that lights the path.

Your Incantations:

_____

_____

_____

Incantation Exercise

Now, set your phone's timer to go off in an hour. When it goes off, incant your phrases ten times.

Each time you incant your phrases, do it with more and more enthusiasm and movement. Don't worry about whether it is working or not. Just do it.

When you finish, put a big smile on your face and praise yourself for having completed the task. Then set your timer again for another hour.

Repeat this process several times throughout the day for three days.

You will be surprised by the increase in energy that you have by the end of the third day. Your words will be fueling your nervous system to release more and more energy. You will feel better about yourself, and you will be creating a powerful internal identity.

The only way that you can do this wrong is to not do it at all. If you feel silly or embarrassed about doing it, then you need this more than you know. Have fun!

CHAPTER 6

The Fourth Element: Kindness

*"People don't care how much you know until
they know how much you care."*
—Theodore Roosevelt

It's been said the thing that sets us apart from animals is that we have the ability to reason. We have the ability to find reasons why to do or not do something. We have the ability to choose what to feel and what not to feel.

Most of the animal kingdom operates purely on instinct. Although it's true that human beings also operate on instinct, we seem to have a stopgap function within our psychology and our nervous system. Even though we get the urge or the temptation to do something, we can choose not to follow our instincts. We can fight off urges and make decisions based on logic and information.

This is, however, a double-edge sword. Sometimes we *know* that following an instinct is not correct, like devouring an entire mound of candy because our instincts think a famine might come soon. But other times, we are taught not to follow instincts that *are* good for us, and for society.

One of the greatest decisions that we can make is the decision to be kind to ourselves, and kind to one another. Kindness is a virtue and virtues feed our souls and enhance everything around us.

My father was an incredibly kind man. Even though he grew up in an era where men tended to be more stoic and macho, my father still went out of his way to be kind to people. He was polite and courteous. I can't ever remember him leaving somebody's presence without him saying "goodbye" or "thank you," or wishing someone well.

I remember one evening being in the car with my father and our whole family. It was freezing cold outside and snowing very hard. My father noticed a man with his family whose car had broken down on the side of the road. My father pulled over and offered the man some help.

As we sat in the car and watched, my dad and the other man worked feverishly under the hood of the man's car. After about 45 minutes, they still couldn't get the car started. I remember seeing my father shake the man's hand and come back to our car. It appeared that my dad wished him well.

My dad got back into the car and as we drove away, I saw the man climb back into his car with his family. My father drove us home and dropped off my mom and siblings. He then gathered all of his tools and put them into the back of our station wagon. He and I went back out and the found man still sitting in his car with his family.

My father then worked with the man for what seemed like a couple of hours. I would get out of the car every once in a while to go see what they were doing, but I couldn't stand the cold, so I'd quickly run back into the car.

Finally, they got the car started. And I remember this like it was yesterday. The man thanked my father over and over again and then offered to pay him for the help that he had given him. My father smiled and said:

"That's OK. You don't owe me anything. You would do the same for me. I'm sure. Pass it on to someone else."

My dad didn't say much on the way home, but I could feel his heart. I could feel that he felt good about what he did, and I could also feel that he felt good that he showed me how to be kind. I never really asked him about it, and we never had an explicit conversation about that evening. But it was clear that this was who my father was. This was part of his integrity.

Throughout my life, I saw my father do many, many other things out of kindness for other people. Whenever anybody would speak harshly, my father would ask: "How would you feel if somebody said that about you?"

Knowing all of this about my father, I have to also mention that my mother was a huge influence in my life as well. She, too, demonstrated all of these characteristics of Magnificence. Especially kindness.

She would do things that she didn't have to do, but she would do them because it was the right thing to do. She loved helping other people. She, too, was always polite. She always said, "please" and "thank you" and wished people well. But more than that, she would embody kindness through her acts of charity and contribution.

Long before it was popular, my mother would organize a basket brigade during the holidays and collect food to give to those in need. I remember when I was about 10 or 11 years old, my mother took me, a boy named Albert Forest, and my older sister out to go door-to-door collecting money for Saint Jude's Children's Hospital.

Growing up, we didn't have much. But there was always somebody out there who didn't have half of what we had. We were raised to believe that it was the right thing to do, and the kind thing to do, to reach out and help others.

I really hated going out and knocking on doors and asking for money. Sometimes people were mean and would slam the door in our faces. Some people would chase us off the porch. It was a thankless job. But mom would always encourage us that we were doing the right thing.

"Not everybody is going to say 'yes,'" she would tell us. "But by you coming into their lives, you caused them to think about something other than themselves. And even though they may not give in that moment, they will realize that somebody else is being kind. In some way, this may shift their thinking."

She always told us even when something *doesn't* feel good at the moment, that may be a sign that you're doing the right thing. I remember coming home from going door-to-door crying a couple of times because I just didn't want to do it anymore. She would hug us and remind us that it's the right thing.

I remember her telling us that kindness is not always easy, but if you continue, it becomes easy. Then the act itself will become the reward. Honestly, at the time I had no idea what she meant. It was confusing. But because she was giving us the opportunity to learn tenacity and discipline, we just kept at it.

After a while, we got so good at fundraising that my sister and I ended up collecting the most money in all of our regions. We were proud of that, but we were prouder that we had done it to help other people.

From middle school through high school, every summer my mom and I would go to the poorest of the poor section of town and somehow convince families to allow her to take care of some of their children for the summer. She would bring home two girls and one boy, and they would live with us for the entire summer. My sisters were responsible for mentoring the girls, and I was responsible for mentoring the boy.

The boy was usually a couple of years younger than me and, as you might imagine, they were thrilled at the opportunity. My mom said that even though we didn't have much at all, these children had less than us and next to nothing. So to them, we were living the dream.

Now *that* was a perspective shift.

At first, I hated it because I wanted to be free and go hang with my friends but I always had this young kid tagging along. Whoever was my companion for the summer, he always looked up to me and followed me everywhere. I got used to it. And that's how we spent our summers. I had to share everything I had and take this younger boy everywhere I went. I had to protect him and teach him.

By the end of the Summer, I remember feeling extremely proud that I was able to show these boys how to do things and give them experiences that they may not have otherwise had. Years later, three of the boys that I had mentored found me and shared with me their lives and what they had become.

Each of them said that they attributed their success in their abundant lives to the times that we spent together. Perhaps the greatest part about the whole thing is that each of them grew up to do the same thing, mentoring others as well.

Nowadays that's called paying it forward. But I just call it kindness.

Even though I sometimes hated doing those things that my parents insisted that we do, there isn't a day that goes by that I don't thank God that they taught us those values. I can honestly say that my life is more fulfilling and more beautiful because I had the privilege of mentoring and teaching others. It continues to be more fulfilling and more beautiful to this day because of the kindness that I learned and was able to spread.

As you approach your dreams, goals, and desires, I invite you to approach them with a spirit of kindness and generosity. Don't do something because you're expecting something back. Do it because it's the right thing to do.

The measure of a person is not simply what they do, but what they do that they *don't have* to do. Judge a person by what they do when nobody's watching.

Be kind to someone else. It doesn't have to cost any money.

Being kind can simply mean giving someone some of your time, attention, and intention. Being kind can be as simple as giving somebody a compliment. It can be as simple as being polite to somebody or saying "please" and "thank you." It can be as simple as giving somebody a smile, some words of encouragement, or a hug.

Kindness Exercise #1

Now, I want you to take some time and brainstorm all the acts of kindness that you have done for others. This list doesn't have to be in chronological order. Just list how you have been kind in the past.

What have you done to help somebody else?

What have you done that has been a simple gesture of kindness?

When was the last time you gave somebody a compliment, or shared some good news with somebody who needed it?

When was the last time you called up a friend just to say hello and wish them well?

When was the last time you hugged someone just because they were there?

When was the last time you told somebody that you loved them?

It takes just a moment to practice these random acts of kindness.

Remember: anything that is repeated will become a habit, and anything that is reinforced will become automatic. This is one of the elements of Magnificence for which the energy you put in is returned to you tenfold.

The more you practice kindness, the better you get at it. The more you practice kindness, the more enhanced your life will become. You will soon find more amazing things flowing toward you.

Treat people the way that you would want to be treated and it will come back in a glorious way.

Your History of Kindness

_____

_____

_____

_____

_____

_____

_____

_____

_____

_____

Be Kind to Yourself

As an ultimate performance specialist, I have had the privilege of working with numerous high-achieving individuals. I have been privileged to work with Academy Award-winning movie stars, Grammy-winning musicians, millionaires, billionaires, politicians, and even royalty.

One of the things that I have noticed is that the majority of them have what I call "the Achiever's Fatal Flaw." You can probably relate to this yourself: they are extremely hard on themselves.

They beat themselves up when they don't achieve what they want. They compare themselves to other people who have gone before them and have achieved many different things. You would be amazed by some of the people who the public views as being certain, confident, and great leaders who actually think the opposite of themselves. I can tell you that the vast majority of these high achievers have issues with regard to how they feel about themselves.

Many of them are kinder to other people than they are to themselves. Again, you can probably relate to this yourself. I know I can.

For many years I felt that if I went easy on myself, then I would be letting myself off the hook and I would slack off. I felt that the best way to get better was to push myself. And I would push myself by comparing myself to others who superficially seemed like they had more and did more than I did.

As it turns out, I was so wrong about this approach.

There is something to be said about pushing oneself because it does produce results. But I can tell you right now that nobody wants to be pushed *all the time.*

Everyone needs to experience kindness as well as discipline. And just like with discipline, the more intense, intentional, and consistent we are in being kind to ourselves, the more powerful the effects will be.

When we push ourselves all the time, at some point, ourselves will push back. This is why we sabotage ourselves.

When we are not congruent with how we feel about ourselves—say, we want to do something, but we don't really believe we are good enough to do it—that's when we start things and don't finish.

If you're telling yourself that you're not good enough or smart enough, that there's something wrong with you, or that you should've done something better than you did, you are sabotaging yourself. When you give yourself that pain, you're literally teaching your nervous system that it is dangerous and painful to try to achieve, and that it's safer to quit and to give up.

So as you approach your dreams, goals, and desires, it is critical that you adopt the behavior of being kind to yourself. Otherwise yourself will never learn how great you are!

This is tough for a lot of people. It can be especially tough for achievers, because we've gotten to where we are by always striving to be better. To tell us to stop and lighten up is like telling us that what we've been doing it wrong all this time.

But I can tell you right now that practicing kindness towards yourself is one of the most important things that you can understand and do to help you go further, faster in your life.

After all, what good is accomplishing something if you feel like crap once you've accomplished it? Worse yet, what if you feel like crap while you're accomplishing it? What does that teach your nervous system about accomplishing things? It certainly doesn't reward it!

The trick is to give all the accolades and appreciation that you possibly can to the most important person in your life: YOU!

Kindness Exercise #2

Take a moment to remember how you have been kind to yourself in the past.

How did you appreciate yourself?

What did you say to yourself about yourself that made you feel good?

What have you done for *you* lately that made you feel proud, lucky, or grateful?

What have you done for YOU lately?

_____

_____

_____

_____

_____

_____

_____

_____

_____

_____

_____

_____

_____

_____

_____

_____

CHAPTER 7

How To Love Anything: Praise

*"If repetition is the mother of all skill, then
praise is the Father."*
— Unknown

Every single living thing responds to positive reinforcement.

When you were a baby, you didn't stand up and run the first time you tried. You didn't say your first words correctly the first time you tried, either.

But whenever you tried, what did your parents do? They encouraged you to keep trying. They gave you love. They gave you appreciation and acknowledgment.

As a result, your nervous system learned that you don't have to get it exactly right. All you have to do is try, and you're going to get the most important emotion that you were put on this planet to feel: Love.

Love is the most rewarding piece of kindness you can give to yourself or anybody else. Your soul craves it from the time you come kicking and screaming onto this earth.

In the back of your mind, even when you are unconscious, the desire to feel love is always there. And the most important person that you want to be loved by is yourself.

Even though human beings are a unique species, we definitely share some physical and mental characteristics with some of our Creator's other Magnificent creatures. For instance, every single organism on the planet comes with a set of built-in instincts. One instinct that we share with all the others is the instinct toward self-preservation.

Even the smallest of creatures will do whatever it takes to survive and fight until the end. Even creatures that are born alone, with no parent to teach or care for them, will instinctively find food, seek safety, and defend themselves. A newborn zebra or gazelle on the Serengeti plains of Africa will struggle to stand only minutes after its birth, all in the effort to preserve the precious gift of life.

Humans are no different. An infant will cry out when it's hungry or alone to summon someone to come and supply it with the basic needs of nourishment and love. This infant instinctively knows that it cannot survive without either one of these necessities.

Another instinct we have is to seek pleasure. Often, things feel good because they are good for us. Sugar and fat taste good because, for millions of years, our ancestors had trouble getting calories, and these high-calorie treats could help them survive. Playing feels good because play is the way we learn important skills like motor skills and social skills. The pull to seek sexual pleasure is the whole basis of procreation for all of us, and for every creature on the planet.

It's natural, it's instinctual, and it's unconscious in all of us to seek pleasure.

What I like to call the "Further, Faster Psychology Technology" is about utilizing our natural, habitual, instinctive behaviors to create new and empowering natural, habitual, instinctive behaviors that serve us. I call this "Contrived Natural Behavior:" the deliberate shaping of the nervous system with the conscious intention and ultimate outcome of producing feelings and behaviors that serve our best interest and the best interest of others.

Since it is a natural instinct to seek pleasure, why don't we apply the Further, Faster process to pleasure-seeking behavior to assist us in getting and staying happier?

Learning a skill comes through repetition. Anything that is repeated enough times will become a habit or a skill. The more you repeat an action, the more your nervous system will become ingrained with that particular movement or emotion. The more ingrained it becomes in your nervous system, the quicker and easier it will become for you to recall and perform that task or process.

Everything with a nervous system shares this characteristic. It is the basic way we all learn. Do anything enough times and you will get good at it. This is how you got good at speaking, walking, driving a car, brushing your teeth, and tying your shoes. This is how you learned everything you do in your life.

This is the reason we practice things: to get good at them. Practice works. It's effective, tried, and true. But while the practice is effective, it is at best the *slower* way of getting good at something.

The way to speed up the process is called Rehearsal. And the way to super speed up the process and turn decades into days is what I call "F.F.R.S." or the "Further, Faster Rehearsal System."

Practice vs. Rehearsal

Practice is simply repeating something over and over until you get better. *Rehearsal* is practice with intense, positive emotion. It is the emotion that stimulates the nervous system to pay attention to what it is being given. So when we do something with intense, positive attention, we are recruiting new parts of our nervous system to the task of learning. We are also making the task its own reward.

It is the emotion which makes the subconscious accept things as real, whether they are or not. It is the emotion which locks your logic and your reasoning into your behavior. And it is positive emotions which tap into that natural instinct to seek pleasure and make us really want to do something even if it was previously uncomfortable. Intense positive emotion makes us crave the process of rehearsal, and in turn speeds up the learning and adaptation process.

Remember this: emotion + repetition = habit.

Excitement. Joy. Enthusiasm. Elation. Surprise. Love. The list goes on and on.

These are all emotions which electrify the nervous system to stand up and take in what is happening while these emotions are taking place. Intensify these emotions and we supercharge the whole rehearsal process, and compress time like crazy.

Here's an analogy: when you are learning to play a classical musical instrument, you first learn scales. The scales are sets of notes that you play over and over again in a specific pattern. The logic is that through repetition, your brain and fingers will sync up and soon you won't have to think about what you are doing. Your body will automatically know what to do when you want to create a specific sound.

This is effective because anything that is repeated will become a pattern. So there you are doing the same thing over and over again, and maybe not really having any fun doing it.

Then all of a sudden, your fingers go somewhere different and it sounds good. You notice this, and you get a little excited because you didn't think it would happen. It just did. This new sound came from out of the blue and it was kind of cool.

So you do it again. And then again. And pretty soon you are playing that new sound or melody on your own. There is excitement and a feeling of accomplishment within you. And it feels good.

What you don't realize is that you now can play something different and you didn't have to go through the same amount of time or effort that you needed to learn the scales. It's already in your nervous system, so you don't have to consciously think about it when you do it.

The point is that when you realized that you did something unique and different, you got excited. As soon as you do that, you ignite your unconscious mind to take in what you just did.

In short, you have amplified the learning process and made it stick in your mind and body. You added a new skill in a fraction of the time it took to achieve similar results through repetitive practice alone.

This is a huge secret to rapid, deep learning. Adapting this process properly will shorten the learning curve for just about anything.

We, as human beings, can direct our emotions and call upon them at will. All we ever need to do is cause ourselves to be excited or happy or joyful or curious.

While we are repeating and learning something, we automatically set in motion the wheels of rapid assimilation and learning. And the same holds true for learning how to consistently feel certain emotions, like happiness and joy, on command.

When we are able to combine the two—repetition with a feeling of happiness, joy, curiosity, or excitement—then we have really cracked the code of our central nervous system.

This is the last piece of the puzzle of Magnificence. It is not last because it is least important; rather, it is last because it is *necessary* for all of the other pieces to stick together with integrity.

I say that because if you do nothing more than this activity alone, you will become much more effective. It is the Rosetta Stone of personal development. It's the one thing that every living thing with a nervous system responds to with rapid, positive, geometric, professional growth.

This final component of Magnificence is called "praise," and it has truly magical powers.

It can turn any bad experience into a good one. It can turn any frown into a smile. It can turn any disappointment into a learning experience. Praise instantly links pleasure whatever just happened, or whatever you just did.

Praise is how you have been trained to do 90% of all of the things that you do and know. The entire nervous system is set up to seek praise, acknowledgment, and appreciation. And because it is always seeking, when it gets that praise, the walls come tumbling down and the grappling hooks of adaptation come flying out.

Why is praise so important to the human nervous system? The first reason is we are designed to seek pleasure like every other animal. That one is a no-brainer. The second reason for all we know is unique only to humans because of the one and only original fear that we are all born with: the fear of being left alone or rejected.

Humans are one of the most social creatures on the planet. Science has now proven that we came to dominate this planet and invent all of the new things we have invented, not because we had the biggest teeth or claws (we certainly don't!) but because we had the best teamwork and the biggest social networks.

What is the difference between Neanderthals (an extinct human species) and *Homo sapiens* which is now by far the most dominant species on planet Earth? Scientists have found that Neanderthals did not trade goods or ideas nearly as enthusiastically as *Homo sapiens*. While Neanderthals only seemed to trade with very nearby families, ancient *Homo sapiens* caves have been found with materials and techniques from *thousands* of miles away.

For a human baby that is left alone, death is almost instant. Even as adults, a single hunter or gatherer—or mom, or computer programmer, for that matter—is going to be in a lot of danger if they are without a tribe. For that reason, the one thing our brains and bodies want *most of all* is affection, approval, and belonging. Our brains know that without these things, we're screwed. So they respond very powerfully when we receive them.

Praise, acknowledgment, and appreciation are all forms of acceptance. And acceptance is what alleviates the fear. So praise powerfully calms our fears, while creating pleasure.

Perhaps it goes without saying that there's a hack to this: *our brain doesn't care where the praise comes from.* Praise that comes from ourselves is just as powerful as praise that comes from others. It is also more reliably available whenever we need to learn, grow, or do something that is uncomfortable but also morally right.

The mechanism in our minds that seeks praise desires not only to experience praise once, but to have it occur as frequently as possible. The nurturing of praise helps keep the ugly, two-headed, green-eyed troll monster called "fear of rejection" asleep in his cave. It ensures this by linking praise to the nearest thing around—especially something that you did.

When you do something and your brain receives praise, your brain makes a simple calculation: "Hey, if I just keep doing that thing, then I will keep getting that feeling that I seek called praise."

This mechanism is so sensitive that you don't even have to get it right every time. Praising anything remotely *close* to your desired activity will do. We aren't focusing on perfection here, but praise.

When a baby turns to the parents and says, "Ma," for the first time, the parents don't ignore or scold the baby because they didn't pronounce the word "mother" properly. Instead they praise, gush over, and reward the baby.

The baby's nervous system, which is the smartest part of any human, begins learning that all they have to do is do it again, and they will get the praise.

The baby knows that they don't have to get it right. They just have to keep trying. And the best part is, they are happy to do it. They experience feel-good emotions while they are doing the task or behavior. They expect that something good will happen when they engage in this behavior, and they are focused on that outcome.

In other words, they are *rehearsing* the behavior. And, as we've covered, rehearsal always produces faster results.

Whenever a human being does something and gets praise for it, this increases their drive to keep doing it. They will begin to perform that behavior unconsciously and willingly. The entire body will engage in orchestrating the dance of activity that will recreate the feeling that it got from the praise.

I hope you can see why *this* is the foundation of all rapid learning and conditioning.

The challenge for most people is that, after a certain age, we stop getting that much-needed praise from others. As we grow up, we are expected to be and do things a certain way without praise. And for the most part, no one teaches us to praise ourselves. Which, by the way, is the best praise of all because it is self-acceptance and we are our own constant companion.

As soon as the slobbering, diseased, hunchbacked, maven of fear of rejection smells the sweet fragrance of self-love and confidence, it quickly runs headlong into the razor-sharp swinging blades of happiness and dies a quick death.

Now, give yourself a round of applause. By now, you are smarter than you were before we met. And it is because you have undertaken the activity of personal development that this is so.

Rehearsal is Activity. Praise is Kindness.

One definition of power is "the ability to make a change." This means that intelligence, knowledge, and information are not enough. At best, they are just *potential* power.

Now you have the knowledge that you need to understand what happiness is and how it works. You also have some knowledge of how you function as a human being, and how you can use that information to get a desired result. Lastly, you have some knowledge and information from our exercises about how you *personally* are set up.

If you have been doing the exercises prescribed in the previous chapters, you have all of the puzzle pieces that you will need to craft and create the happiness that you picked this book up for in the first place.

You should have a strong association with the word Magnificent; great feelings from the items you listed in our exercise; and a smile on your face (even if you don't think you do).

If you have been doing what I asked, you still have all of the positive emotions we have created throughout this book. And they *will* serve you well.

We all *know* things, but we don't always *apply* what we know. With the best of intentions our psyche rationalizes, deletes, distorts, and justifies the behaviors that hold us back at the threshold of happiness, achievement, and success.

We all know how to lose weight. All you need to do at the end of the day is spend more calories than you consume. There are thousands of diets out there that make this easier, and millions of people that have successfully done it.

The know-how is there. Know-how is a plentiful commodity. What is *not* so plentiful is something called "wisdom."

Wisdom is applied knowledge. Wisdom is knowledge that is *acted on* until results occur. And the only way to get wisdom is through experience.

So that is what we are about to do. We are about to put together all of the puzzle pieces and perform a strategy that will produce results.

Keep in mind, you don't have to get it right the first time or even the second, third, or fourth to deserve kindness from yourself. More kindness means more motivation to continue. And that means giving yourself more praise for your rehearsals.

CHAPTER 8

The Fifth Element: Joy

"When you do things from your soul, you feel a river moving in you, a joy."
— Rumi

Out of all the elements of Magnificence that I learned from my father, joyfulness is the one that has served me best. There are so many benefits to having this as part of your personality and your foundational operating system.

To be clear, "joyfulness" does not just mean having a perpetual smile on your face and only looking at the bright side of things. We all need to process painful emotions and losses sometimes. But joyfulness is a way of thinking, moving, and feeling that can even penetrate the ways that we grieve and get angry. It's actually a skill that is perfected over time.

Although it's true that some people seem to be naturally joyful, I assure you that they have their ups and downs as well. Somewhere along the way, they *learned* how to be joyful. Although it may be true that some of us coming into this world are predisposed to have a joyful nature about us, it is certain that our demeanor and behaviors were reinforced in such a way that we were encouraged to make them a permanent part of who we are.

My father, Joseph McClendon Jr., was one of those individuals. Despite the fact that he grew up in one of the harshest environments in the United States in the '20s, '30s, and '40s, he came through it full of joy and laughter.

He was genuinely a happy guy. He loved to laugh and was one of the silliest grown men I have ever known. My father would laugh so hard sometimes that tears would roll down his face. Even if you didn't know what he was laughing about or didn't get the joke, you couldn't be around him and not laugh yourself.

I remember many times as a young boy seeing my father burst out laughing, and I would immediately start laughing too.

Even though I had no clue on this God's green earth what we were laughing about.

I would watch other people around my father. When he was around, they would light up and become more animated and engaged. Along with his politeness and his generosity and his integrity, he was an unstoppable force for good in people's lives.

My father wasn't much for telling jokes or being funny, but his energy was joyful and fun. You could tell that he appreciated life. If something wasn't fun, he would make it fun.

I remember when he was studying and going to night school, he was really into mathematics. He would come home and have to do homework, but he made it into a game.

My father would sit down at the dinner table with a legal pad and a mechanical pencil and write out problems for hours. In those days there were no handheld computers or calculators. The only thing that was available were those bulky adding machines, and they were expensive. So he made it fun by going out and buying a simple abacus instead.

He figured out how to use this ancient tool like a puzzle, and he used it to make his homework fun and entertaining while still getting the job done.

As you approach your journey toward your dreams, goals, and desires, do so with a spirit of joyfulness. Optimism and levity make the journey worth traveling.

It's been said thousands of times that time flies by when you're having fun. So as long as you're going to be doing anything at all, look for ways to make it fun and joyful. Look for things to laugh at and with.

Looking for joy, just like looking for anything else, will create more of it. The expectation is half the fun, and the bounty is infinitely more rewarding when the journey is filled with joy, laughter, and love. There are several fringe benefits and spinoffs that come with being joyful as well.

Any and everything that you want in life is going to involve other people. People will want to be around people that are joyful. Spreading joy to other people is like a domino effect.

In my previous book, "Get Happy Now," I mention several studies in the field of psychoneuroimmunology. In one study, the scientists analyzed the effects of laughter, joy, and happiness and how they affected the subject's mental and physical well-being.

Among many other favorable benefits, they discovered that one minute of anger weakens your immune system for four to five hours. But one minute of laughter, of being joyful, produces endorphins and other hormones in your body that strengthen your immune system for over 24 hours.

Laughter actually is the best medicine. Being joyful, being kind and energetic while having tenacity and living from a place of integrity actually creates a cybernetic, perpetual loop that enhances every part of our spiritual, mental, and physical being.

These are the five essential elements of greatness.

Joyfulness Is A Thought Process

In 1988, our family received some devastating news. My mother was diagnosed with stage four terminal cancer in her intestine. The doctors operated and took out two-thirds of the tumor, but they had to leave the remaining third in. Otherwise, the surgery would have taken her life on the spot.

After the surgery, the doctors stitched her up, made her comfortable, and then came to us and told us that her life expectancy was about 60 days. They told us that it would be best to get her affairs in order and prepare for her passing.

Fortunately, my friend Dr. Deepak Chopra had shared with me something a few weeks earlier that changed everything. He said that seven to eight times out of ten, when the patient is told that they have a terminal disease and they have a certain amount of time to live, the patient passes away on or very, very close to the time period.

If the physician says they have two months to live, right around 60 days the person expires. Deepak told me that if you're ever given a prognosis of inevitable death within a timeframe, that you should reply and believe in your heart: "Doctor, I appreciate your diagnosis, but I will not accept your verdict."

About a year earlier, I'd heard about and read some of the work of a Doctor Norman Cousins. Dr. Cousins had healed himself from a terminal disease and helped other people to heal themselves through laughter.

My mother, who was a joyful person already set out to do the same. Even before she left the hospital, we were watching videos, telling jokes, laughing, and remaining positive and optimistic.

She did have to go through some pretty hard times. It was very painful and difficult. But in the end, my mother lived another eleven and a half years and she was cancer-free for eight of those years.

The world is full of examples of people who changed their health through laughter and joyfulness.

Laughter causes us to use our diaphragm to breathe deeply. As a result, we take in more oxygen. We move our bodies as we do so. This generates more energy and fortifies the immune system to attack whatever is going on inside of our bodies.

Unfortunately, when people hear that they have some sort of ailment, they often stop being optimistic and start being pessimistic. This taxes their nervous system and immune system. This type of stress runs rampant when others around us are concerned and become bearers of bad news as well.

The trick to life is to allow yourself the pleasure of being joyful. It's always an option, and it's always a choice.

How To Choose Joy

Even though it might sound Pollyanna and overly simplistic, joyfulness is a skill. And as with any skill, it can be taught and learned. It can also be conditioned into our nervous systems so that it becomes a natural extension of who we are.

Yes, you're hearing and reading this right. I am right here in front of God and everybody saying that you can change your disposition and your personality.

Remember, anything that is repeated will become a habit. Any habit that is positively reinforced will become an automatic and conditioned response.

Also remember that the brain, the body, and the heart cannot resist repetition. This is exactly how you were wired growing up, and exactly how you have created the life, the lifestyle, and emotional well-being that you have right now.

Lastly, there is a way to speed up the process so that it doesn't have to take a lifetime to create a shift in this area. The only reason I didn't put this as the *first* virtue and element of Magnificence is that most people might think this as being too soft or too metaphysical. But the reality is that integrity, tenacity, energy, and kindness are all direct spin-offs from joyfulness. Each and every one of the other elements on this list is enhanced by this quality.

Earlier in this book, we talked about the mechanics of how humans function. I gave the example of an automobile engine, how it starts, and how it continues to run.

Our emotions are set up in a similar fashion. Every emotion that we experience is a result of a sequence of physical components which work together to produce a specific emotion. I call this "Emotional Mechanics," and it works like clockwork every single time you have any emotion at all.

Having this information allows you to alter the sequence of motion and mechanics and produce any desired emotion that you want. In addition, you can cause that syntax to be natural and automatic so that it becomes one of your personality traits and behaviors.

A simple example of this is a smile. When we smile, we employ several of the eighty muscles in our face to produce that smile.

Remember, each muscle movement carries with it a release of electricity and energy that courses through our bodies. In addition, that physical movement causes several of our glands to release hormones that actually make us *feel* happy. The very movement causes our brain to release endorphins and dopamine, which in turn causes oxytocin to release adrenaline and a whole host of other solutions which I like to simply call "awesome sauce."

Joy Exercise

What brings you joy? These are the things you want to make sure you have in your life on a daily basis. It can be anything from a funny TV show to a game, social activity, self-praise, a particular outfit, a particular color, or any daily ritual or happening that you really enjoy.

For the next ten minutes, I want you to write down—yes, with a pen or pencil—everything you can think of that brings you joy. This will become your "resource handbook" for joy.

Just by writing these things down, you will be more mindful of them and more likely to incorporate them into your life in the future. If you want, you can make a list of items to make sure you incorporate into your daily routine.

What Brings You Joy?

_____

_____

_____

_____

_____

_____

_____

_____

_____

CHAPTER 9

You've Got It Now

*"The spoils go to those few who not only chose
to do the mental, physical, and emotional work; but
who also do the work consistently. This is the law."*
—Joseph McClendon III

What is 'It?'

"The 'it' girl." "He's got it going on." "She's really got it."

We hear a lot about 'it.' 'It' is a seemingly indefinable quality that everyone just loves. The people who have 'it' seem to be popular, charismatic, confident, and desired. They are 'naturals' at whatever skill they excel in. They are gracious and graceful. They seem to succeed at everything they do. They must have popped out of the womb confident and charismatic.

What is that thing that we've all heard about our whole lives, that some people are "born with" and others don't think they have?

The first time I remember hearing about 'it' was when my older sister and I entered our school talent show.

Neither one of us really wanted to enter, because even at thirteen and fourteen, we thought it was a bit goofy and uncool. That's what we told ourselves and our parents, anyway. Truth be told, we were both just plain old afraid. We were afraid of screwing up in front of the whole school and being marked as dorks for all eternity.

At the time, I thought it was just me who was afraid. Later in life, I found out that my big sister Ava was frightened too. This was a revelation for me because I always thought my big sister had 'it.' How could she be scared of anything? How could she ever fear being embarrassed?

You see, my big sister was amazing in my eyes. She was funny, fun, and outgoing. Everyone seemed to like her instantly. She could walk into a room and everyone would immediately notice that she was there. Later she actually became our school mascot and was voted most popular in the school yearbook. She was talented and extremely bright.

I, on the other hand, was a bit nerdy, shy, unsure of myself. In my awkward and painfully self-conscious pre-teen years, I sported some of the lowest self-esteem on record. I felt for sure that my sister had 'it' and I didn't.

Looking back, though, I now realize she was just as scared as I was. I also realize that I was really creative, good with my hands, and a pretty good piano player.

My mother convinced us to enter this talent show saying that it would help us to build character and gain more confidence and certainty about our abilities.

She once told us that if you have a gift or a talent, you owe it to yourself and to all of the people who helped you along the way to express that gift or talent. She used to say, "You don't just do something just for the fun of it. You also do it to share it with others to make their lives richer and better."

My sister and I decided to do a comedy skit that my sister had created where she played a beautiful opera singer preparing to sing her song, and I was her pianist accompanying her. She would begin to sing her song and I would fumble, and bumble up the beginning over and over again, causing her great embarrassment.

Each time we would start again it got worse and worse. And each time she would get angrier and angrier at me but would have to keep her game face and her composure for the audience.

She would scoff at me for screwing up and then quickly smile apologetically at the audience. I would do the same but would screw up even bigger the next time. Finally, we would get it together and when we actually played the song, the audience would be doubly surprised because she could really sing, and I could really play.

That was the theory, anyway. But as the day approached, we worried about whether we would really be able to pull it off.

There was no dress rehearsal, so none of the other acts knew what we were doing. The school just called an assembly in the gymnasium in front of the whole school, and we all had to just go for it.

I was so terrified that I felt like I was going to lose my lunch just before we went on stage. We were to be the third from the last act, and there were some really great acts before us.

Even though I thought the other acts were awesome and I genuinely appreciated and even rooted for them, deep down my certainty was growing that my sister and I would do an outstanding job.   I knew that we had something unique, and that my sister would win their hearts.

The funny thing is, I don't actually remember much about being onstage and performing. The only thing I really remember was hitting the last note on the piano and hearing my sister's voice ringing out along with that note. Then, silence.

Even though the silence only lasted about two seconds, it seemed like thirty minutes. The audience had applauded immediately for all of the other acts. But for us...*nothing.*

I stood up and took my beautiful sister by the hand. I was trembling, but she was not. We took a bow and turned to walk offstage.

And then it happened. The audience went crazy. They jumped to their feet and started screaming and yelling with joy. I was floored. I'd thought that they hated us, and that I was destined to finish my high school years labeled as a complete jackass.

In the end, we actually won the talent show and my school popularity stock went up! The interesting thing was that for some time after that, people kept telling us, "You two really have 'it.'" They seemed to think we had something special that they didn't have.

They'd say things like "you two are naturals," and "you made it look so easy." People would say that we seemed so confident and sure of ourselves.

To my core, I remember thinking that they just don't know. They didn't know how my guts were turning before the event, or how much I doubted myself. They didn't know that my sister and I hadn't even wanted to participate in the first place because we were afraid of failing. They didn't know about all of the anxiety proceeding the show.

I never said anything, but I wanted them to know that there really wasn't anything special about us. All I knew was that we had put in the work and *prepared*.

I believe that everyone has 'it.' 'It' is not something you are born with, but something that you learn through rehearsal just like when my sister and I rehearsed at home.

What is 'it?!' It's the *zone*. The flow. The clear space where time flies by and stands still all at the same time. It's that coveted feeling of certainty and confidence that *you've got this*, and no matter what happens, you will be the victor. It's that effortless effort-ing that feels natural and even comfortable to the point that you don't even remember doing it.

Nobody is born with *it*. We acquire it through rehearsal. And how do we acquire a love of rehearsal? Think back over the last few chapters.

That's right. We acquire a love of rehearsal by being *praised* when we rehearse. Rehearsing, and achieving great results, then becomes a self-sustaining cycle.

My sister and I were lucky enough to have a mother who encouraged us to rehearse, and praised us when we did it, from an early age. As a result we were able to give the appearance of having 'it' at an early age as well.

You might not have the same head start. Maybe your parents didn't encourage or reward you in this way. But you can learn remarkably fast when you rehearse properly in the ways we've discussed in this book. It's never too late to give yourself the gift of 'it' in the area of your choosing.

Everyone has something that they do well. Everyone has been in the *zone* where we could do no wrong. The ball bounces perfectly in our direction, we say just the right thing, we perform flawlessly, and we excel beyond the competition and the masses.

Whatever it is that you wish to do in your life from this point forward, know that you have what it takes to be the best. You have access to that 'it' anytime you need it. *And* you have the ability to make that 'it' show up automatically and organically without having to sweat it every time.

I do want to point out that this book is not the end-all and be-all to master your performance forever. You are going to have to work at building the skills in this book, and the skills and muscles particular to your life goals, beyond these exercises.

But think of this book as the key. Now that you have the knowledge contained within these pages, you know exactly *how* and *why* to train yourself so that you love rehearsing, you accelerate your learning, and you develop 'it' in every area that you choose.

Just remember: knowledge isn't power. It is only *potential* power. Real power—the kind that makes the real world turn—comes from action and activity.

Remember, your brain cannot resist repetition. It does not judge for itself what is true or not true. It will always act upon the thoughts, feelings, and words that you hand it. This is where your brain gets its beliefs about you, about what is easy or difficult for you to do, about what you do or don't enjoy doing and what you are or are not good at.

You can shape those beliefs any way you want with just a little time and conscious strategy.

Here are some of my own personal favorite praises and incantations. Feel free to borrow mine, or make up some of your own:

1. I am gaining more and more reasons to be happier than ever.

2. I am grateful beyond measure.

3. I am Magnificent in every way.

4. I am uniquely qualified to be the best.

5. I love life and life loves me.

6. I freaking ROCK.

7. I have so much to be thankful for.

8. I am peaceful and centered.

9. I am excited to experience what the future holds.

10. I choose to be happy every day.

11. I love to laugh at myself and share joy.

12. My smile and joy touch everyone around me.

13. My happiness creates more happiness geometrically.

14. My happiness attracts more and more blessings into my life.

15. Every day in every way I'm growing happier and happier.

16. Happiness is my birthright and I claim more and more of it every single day.

17. I spread happiness to others and absorb happiness from others.

18. My happiness makes all others see how blessed they are.

19. I enjoy my life and my happiness is real.

20. I happily interact with others, knowing I am enhancing their lives.

21. Each and every day I am happily moving closer to my dreams, goals, and desires.

22. I am thankful to everybody who has touched my life and I wish them deep happiness.

23. Happy thoughts are the foundation of my subconscious.

24. I live, love, and laugh through my life every day.

25. I love my life and all that I am.

26. I make myself happy just by being me.

27. I am happy to be alive.

28. I radiate love, joy, and unconditional happiness.

29. I graciously accept love, wealth, health, and happiness in my life.

30. I deserve love, joy and beauty and I happily accept it all.

31. I am kind. I am loving, joyful, grateful. I am happy.

32. As I seek happiness it finds me.

33. My thoughts and dreams are grounded in happiness.

34. My heart and soul are magnets to joy and happiness.

35. I am overwhelmed with gratitude for the joy that fills my life.

36. I live my life with positive expectations.

37. I accept the good that is flowing into my life.

38. Happiness and more happiness is mine.

39. Happiness is everywhere I look. As I look I see, hear, and feel more of it.

40. Happy thoughts bring happy things.

41. I smile and my life lightens.

42. This very minute more and more happiness is dancing its way into my life.

43. Every day I experience unlimited joy and happiness.

44. Happiness follows and leads me through life always.

45. I am filled with happiness and I spread it to everyone that crosses my path.

46. Every day I am healing, healthy, wealthy, and happy.

47. Every day I am getting happier and happier and all that I desire is gaining on me.

48. I gratefully accept all of the wealth and happiness that the Universe pours into me every day.

49. I am love. I am abundance. I am joy. I am living happiness.

50. With every breath I take, the universe is providing for my every want and need.

51. I am at peace and happiness with myself now.

52. Everything that I do sends joy, love, and happiness to the universe and it responds with the same back to me.

CHAPTER 10

North Star in Times of Trouble

"Dream the biggest dream for yourself. Hold the highest vision of life for yourself."
— Oprah Winfrey

"Man, alone can transform the power of his thoughts into physical reality; man, alone can dream, and make his dream come true."
— Napoleon Hill

It's been exactly 67 days now since my life and the lives of most of the rest of us living on this planet have been forever changed.

What started out as a simple stay-at-home recommendation has turned into a full-on quarantine with masks, gloves, and social distancing. Overnight, life as we once knew it turned on a dime and came to a screeching halt.

My life has gone from traveling internationally at the very least 10 days per month to not traveling any further than the 2 ½ miles that it takes to get to the grocery store from my home.

I went from standing in front of 10 to 15,000 people live on stage each month to zero overnight.

I am sure that similar, seemingly catastrophic changes have come for many of you. Maybe you have lost your job, taken a pay cut, or been furloughed because your business can't do business as usual. Maybe you are still being required to go out to work, and you worry about becoming infected with the virus that's going around. Maybe you are struggling between your desire to stay safe and your desire to pay your rent or mortgage.

But the good news is, we are all in this together. None of us is alone.

And one of the things that sets the most successful people apart is this: when one door closes, they see another door open.

Think about it. The danger of getting wrapped up in our expectations is this: if something changes so what we once planned is no longer possible, it's easy to feel devastated. It's easy to feel that life is unfair. It's easy to feel that all is lost, because now you aren't going to be able to do that thing you were going to do.

But what can you do now that you *couldn't* do before?

What options are now open because Plan A has been closed off—at least for now?

What can you do with the freedom and time you now have, since you can't be required to go to work every day?

At a higher level, we can ask ourselves: what changes are possible for our *society* now? How might we harness the changes the pandemic has brought to create a kinder, more fair, more cooperative future? What space has opened up to build new habits, new thought patterns, and new ways of relating to each other?

Do you remember at the beginning of this book when we wrote about our past, present, and desired *future* beliefs about ourselves? Do you remember when we talked about what you would ideally *like* to believe about yourself in the future if you could choose anything?

We're going to do that same exercise again now. Except this time, we're going to write about what we desire for the whole *world* in the future.

Question #1: What Do You Want?

What do you want? Why did you pick up this book? Think about what you want for the whole world, as well as your individual goals.

_____

_____

_____

Question #2: How Will You Feel When You Have It?

How will you feel when the change you want to see has happened?
What will you be able to do with your newfound bounty?
Will you feel relieved and satisfied? Will you be excited and motivated?

_____

_____

_____

_____

_____

_____

_____

_____

_____

_____

_____

_____

_____

_____

Question #3: How Will You Make This Happen?

Now, what are some actions you can take to *make this happen* in the next day? In the next week? In the next month?

Big changes in the world are made of little changes people make, so create your strategy to make your dream a reality. It's okay to start small.

_____

_____

_____

_____

_____

_____

_____

_____

_____

_____

_____

_____

_____

The people who are able to take advantage of the changes that have been handed to us are the people who will come out of this ahead in advancing whatever goals they might have for themselves and for the world. And I hope that one of these people will be you.

Be the change you want to see. Now more than ever, we are reminded how much integrity, tenacity, energy, kindness, and joy. For our individual Magnificence, and for the Magnificence of our society.

Of course, one of the things we all need to do right now is grieve. This is no small task.

Our bodies and emotions are physical entities: they have inertia. We cannot simply switch gears and decide not to care about something we cared about before. Instead, there is a process we must experience to let go of old expectations before we can welcome the new. This process is called grieving.

It's okay to be sad some of the time. In fact, sadness is necessary. How else would we know what joy feels like?

It's okay to be angry some of the time. In fact, anger exists to motivate us. How else would we know when we need to fight to make things better?

Life is change. Changing states, changing abilities, and changing possibilities.

If you find yourself stuck in an emotional state that you don't want to be in anymore, I hope this book will be of service to you in changing the way you view yourself and your possibilities. I hope it will help you have the tools that you need to choose the experiences that you want to have in life.

If you're just surviving in the face of mental health or medical challenges, that's something too. That's something really big. Surviving is our first duty, to ourselves and to everyone else.

It is my hope that this book will help you to survive, and to thrive, even in the midst of changing times.

It is my hope that having the ability to change and choose your beliefs about yourself and the world will empower you to become like many of my clients: the best in their chosen fields.

It is my hope that *all* of us will make the choices needed to build a brighter, kinder, more resilient future.

And it is my honor to have guided you on this journey. I hope I have succeeded, in some small measure, in sharing with you what my father once shared with me.

More Books by Joseph McClendon III

Awesome Sauce

Awesome Sauce is what I call the mix of hormones and chemicals released by the brain and the body release when we are operating at our absolute best. This book teaches you to master your own special Awesome Sauce at will.

Change Your Breakfast, Change Your Life

Feel better, have more energy, look younger and be healthier NOW! If you want to radically affect the aging process, increase your energy levels, control your emotions, increase your fitness, and lose weight, then this book by Joseph McClendon III is a must-read for you.

Get Happy NOW

Get Happy in 10 Minutes. Feel Happy in 10 Days. Be Happy for Life! How can increasing your happiness change everything about your life? Joseph McClendon, a global life transformation and practicing neuropsychologist, brings new tools and a fresh perspective to help you reach the next higher level of happiness. Joseph arms the reader with the tactics and techniques to think and grow rich, abundant, and happy relationships and businesses.

Ebony Power Thoughts

The power within the words of our great black leaders and role models is astonishing. By studying their positive accomplishments, we can move forward to our own successes. In Ebony Power Thoughts you will find the words you need as tools for growth and fulfillment, with questions you can use as assistance in benefitting your own life.

About the Author

Joseph McClendon III is a Doctor of Neuropsychology and one of the most sought after Ultimate Performance Specialists in the industry.

His unique brand of Tell, Show, Do teaching and coaching creates rapid personal change that effectively moves people to take more consistent action and go Further Faster with their personal and business achievements.

Joseph holds several certifications in the neurosciences arena. He taught at the University of California Los Angeles (UCLA) for seven years and is frequently called upon to lecture at other higher learning institutions like Harvard University and many Fortune 500 companies in the United States as well as across Europe and Australia.

Joseph has delivered hundreds of workshops, coaching sessions, keynote addresses, seminars and training programs, and one-on-one therapeutic interventions and has presented to well over 3 million people around the globe. His remarkable ability to go straight to the core of the challenge and effect rapid change makes him a unique commodity in business, health and wellness, and personal improvement.

Made in United States
North Haven, CT
25 April 2023

35846295R00102